Mastering Commercial Law

Your Ultimate Guide to Understanding Key Business Structures and Terms Related To Sole Proprietorships, Partnerships, and Corporations Like A Pro In Minutes.

-- By Louis Coleman --

Text Copyright © by Louis Coleman

All rights reserved. No part of this guide may be reproduced in any form without permission in writing from the publisher except in the case of brief quotations embodied in critical articles or reviews.

Legal & Disclaimer

The information contained in this book and its contents is not designed to replace or take the place of any form of medical or professional advice; and is not meant to replace the need for independent medical, financial, legal or other professional advice or services, as may be required. The content and information in this book have been provided for educational and entertainment purposes only.

The content and information contained in this book have been compiled from sources deemed reliable, and it is accurate to the best of the Author's knowledge, information, and belief. However, the Author cannot guarantee its accuracy and validity and cannot be held liable for any errors and/or omissions. Further, changes are periodically made to this book as and when needed. Where appropriate and/or necessary, you must consult a professional (including but not limited to your doctor, attorney, financial advisor or such other professional advisor) before using any of the suggested remedies, techniques, or information in this book.

Upon using the contents and information contained in this book, you agree to hold harmless the Author from and against any damages, costs, and expenses, including any legal fees potentially resulting from the application of any of the information provided by this book. This disclaimer applies to any loss, damages or injury caused by the use and application, whether directly or indirectly, of any advice or information presented, whether for breach of contract, tort, negligence, personal injury, criminal intent, or under any other cause of action.

You agree to accept all risks of using the information presented inside this book.

You agree that by continuing to read this book, where appropriate and/or necessary, you shall consult a professional (including but not limited to your doctor, attorney, or financial advisor or such other advisor as needed) before using any of the suggested remedies, techniques, or information in this book.

TABLE OF CONTENTS

INTRODUCTION 5

EXPLORE THREE PRIMARY TYPES OF BUSINESS STRUCTURES: SOLE PROPRIETORSHIP, PARTNERSHIP, AND CORPORATION 7

COMMON LEGAL TERMS IN BUSINESS - PART ONE 11

SOLE PROPRIETORSHIP: WHAT IT IS, ITS ADVANTAGES AND DISADVANTAGES, AND HOW IT FUNCTIONS 20

A HYPOTHETICAL CONVERSATION BETWEEN A LAWYER AND A CLIENT WHO IS SEEKING ADVICE ON CHOOSING THE BEST BUSINESS STRUCTURE 24

A CONVERSATION BETWEEN A LAWYER AND A CLIENT, FOCUSING ON THE BENEFITS AND DRAWBACKS OF SETTING UP A BUSINESS AS A SOLE PROPRIETOR 29

EXPLORE SOME CRITICAL QUESTIONS TO CONSIDER WHEN CHOOSING A BUSINESS STRUCTURE AND MANAGING LEGAL ASPECTS OF YOUR BUSINESS 34

A PARTNERSHIP: WHAT IT IS, ITS TYPES, ADVANTAGES, AND DISADVANTAGES 39

A CONVERSATION BETWEEN A LAWYER AND A CLIENT WHO IS CONSIDERING FORMING A PARTNERSHIP FOR THEIR NEW BUSINESS 44

A CONVERSATION BETWEEN A LAWYER AND A CLIENT WHO HAS QUESTIONS ABOUT CREATING A PARTNERSHIP AGREEMENT FOR A NEW BUSINESS 49

COMMON LEGAL TERMS USED IN THE CONTEXT OF PARTNERSHIPS: PART TWO 54

A CORPORATION: WHAT IT IS, ITS KEY CHARACTERISTICS, ADVANTAGES, AND DISADVANTAGES 65

A CONVERSATION BETWEEN A LAWYER AND A CLIENT WHO IS CONSIDERING STARTING A CORPORATION FOR THEIR NEW BUSINESS 69

EXPLORE THE KEY BENEFITS AND CHALLENGES OF FORMING A CORPORATION 74
CONCLUSION 79
CHECK OUT OTHER BOOKS 82

INTRODUCTION

Welcome to **"Mastering Commercial Law: Your Ultimate Guide to Understanding Key Business Structures and Terms Related To Sole Proprietorships, Partnerships, and Corporations Like A Pro In Minutes."**

In a world where businesses drive innovation and progress, understanding the legal frameworks that underpin them is not just an asset; it is a necessity. Whether you are an aspiring entrepreneur, a seasoned business owner, or someone fascinated by the intricacies of commercial law, **this book is your gateway** to mastering the critical concepts that shape the business world.

Why This Book?

Imagine being equipped with the knowledge to navigate the complexities of business law with ease and confidence. Picture yourself making informed decisions that safeguard your interests and propel your business forward. This book is designed to be **your trusted companion** on this journey, demystifying the legal landscape and providing you with the tools to make sound, strategic choices.

What Will You Gain?

In-Depth Understanding of Business Structures: From the simplicity of a sole proprietorship to the intricate dynamics of partnerships and the robust framework of corporations, we will explore each business structure in detail. You will discover their unique advantages, potential pitfalls, and the critical factors to consider when choosing the best fit for your venture.

Mastery of Legal Vocabulary: Legal jargon can often seem like a foreign language. In this book, we break down complex legal terms into simple, easy-to-understand concepts. By the end of your reading, you will be fluent in the language of business law, equipped to engage confidently in legal discussions and negotiations.

Practical Insights and Real-World Examples: Theory is important, but practical application is crucial. This guide is packed with real-world examples that illustrate the concepts in action, providing you with a practical understanding that goes beyond the textbook. Learn from the successes and challenges of real businesses as you navigate your own path.

Why Should You Care?

In the fast-paced world of business, the stakes are high. Making uninformed decisions can lead to costly mistakes, legal battles, and missed opportunities. By mastering the principles of commercial law, you are not just protecting your business; you are positioning it for success. You will gain the confidence to tackle complex legal issues, seize opportunities, and steer your business towards growth and sustainability.

Who Is This Book For?

Whether you are launching a startup, expanding an existing business, or simply curious about how businesses operate within the legal framework, this book is for you. It is designed to be accessible, engaging, and highly informative, making complex legal concepts approachable and easy to grasp.

How to Use This Book

Each chapter is crafted to build your knowledge step-by-step. Start with an overview of business structures, then delve into the specifics of sole proprietorships, partnerships, and corporations. As you progress, you will encounter key legal terms explained in plain language, supported by practical examples and case studies. Use this book as a reference guide, a learning tool, and a source of inspiration as you navigate the world of commercial law.

Let's Get Started

Are you ready to master the legal foundations of business and elevate your understanding of commercial law? Are you prepared to unlock the potential that lies within the knowledge of business structures and legal terminology? Dive in, and let this journey transform the way you think about and approach business law.

Welcome to the world of commercial law. Welcome to your ultimate guide to mastering it.

EXPLORE THREE PRIMARY TYPES OF BUSINESS STRUCTURES: SOLE PROPRIETORSHIP, PARTNERSHIP, AND CORPORATION

Introduction

Welcome to the world of Commercial Law! In this chapter, we will delve into the different types of business structures that are fundamental to understanding commercial operations. Whether you are a budding entrepreneur, a student of law, or simply curious about how businesses are organized, this guide will simplify the complexities of commercial law and provide clear, practical examples.

Understanding the types of business structures is crucial for making informed decisions about starting or managing a business. Each type has unique characteristics, benefits, and legal implications that can significantly impact how a business operates and grows. We will explore three primary types of business structures: Sole Proprietorship, Partnership, and Corporation.

1. Sole Proprietorship

A **sole proprietorship** is the simplest and most common form of business ownership. It is owned and operated by one individual, and there is no legal distinction between the owner and the business. This means that the owner is personally responsible for all the debts and obligations of the business.

Advantages:

- **Ease of Formation**: Setting up a sole proprietorship is straightforward and involves minimal legal paperwork.
- **Control**: The owner has complete control over business decisions and operations.
- **Tax Benefits**: The business income is reported on the owner's personal tax return, which can simplify tax filing and potentially offer tax advantages.

Disadvantages:

- **Unlimited Liability**: The owner is personally liable for all business debts and legal actions.
- **Limited Capital**: Raising funds can be challenging, as it relies primarily on the owner's personal resources.

- **Continuity Issues**: The business does not continue if the owner decides to retire or passes away.

Example: Imagine Sarah, who loves baking, decides to start her own bakery called "Sarah's Sweets." She sets up a sole proprietorship, meaning she is the sole owner and responsible for all aspects of the business. If Sarah's Sweets incurs debt, Sarah is personally liable to pay it off, even if it means using her personal savings.

2. Partnership

A **partnership** involves two or more individuals who agree to share the profits, losses, and responsibilities of running a business. Partnerships can be further categorized into General Partnerships and Limited Partnerships.

General Partnership: All partners share equal responsibility for the management of the business and its liabilities.

Limited Partnership: Includes both general partners, who manage the business and are personally liable for its debts, and limited partners, who contribute capital but have limited liability and typically do not participate in day-to-day operations.

Advantages:

- **Shared Responsibility**: Partners can pool resources and share the workload, which can be beneficial for business growth.
- **Combined Skills**: Each partner brings unique skills and expertise, enhancing the business's overall capabilities.
- **Tax Benefits**: Partnerships benefit from pass-through taxation, meaning business income is reported on the partners' personal tax returns.

Disadvantages:

- **Joint Liability**: Partners are jointly liable for the business's debts and obligations, which can expose them to significant personal risk.
- **Potential for Conflict**: Differences in opinions and goals among partners can lead to disputes and affect the business's stability.
- **Profit Sharing**: Profits must be shared among partners, which can reduce the individual share of income.

Example: Consider Alex and Jamie, who decide to start a consulting firm together. They form a general partnership called "AJ Consulting." Both contribute capital and expertise to the business. If AJ Consulting faces a lawsuit, both Alex and Jamie could be held personally responsible for any legal judgments, risking their personal assets.

3. Corporation

A **corporation** is a more complex business structure that is legally separate from its owners, who are shareholders. Corporations can raise capital by issuing shares and are governed by a board of directors.

Advantages:

- **Limited Liability**: Shareholders are only liable for the amount they invested in the corporation, protecting their personal assets from business liabilities.
- **Perpetual Existence**: Corporations continue to exist even if the owners change or pass away.
- **Capital Acquisition**: Corporations can raise significant capital by selling shares, which can fuel expansion and growth.

Disadvantages:

- **Complex Formation**: Setting up a corporation requires more legal paperwork, regulatory compliance, and costs.
- **Double Taxation**: Corporations may face double taxation, where profits are taxed at the corporate level and again when distributed as dividends to shareholders.
- **Regulatory Requirements**: Corporations are subject to strict regulatory requirements and reporting standards.

Example: Let's take the example of Tech Innovations Inc., a technology startup that develops innovative software solutions. As a corporation, Tech Innovations can issue shares to investors to raise capital for research and development. If the company faces financial difficulties, the personal assets of the shareholders, including its founders, are protected from business debts.

Conclusion

Understanding the different types of business structures is essential for anyone interested in the world of commerce. Each structure has its unique features, advantages, and disadvantages that can influence a business's operations and success. Whether you choose a sole proprietorship for its simplicity, a partnership for its collaborative benefits, or a corporation for its growth potential and liability protection, it is important to consider the legal and financial implications of each option.

COMMON LEGAL TERMS IN BUSINESS - PART ONE

Introduction

Welcome to the first chapter on Legal Vocabulary in our guide to understanding Commercial Law. This chapter aims to demystify common legal terms that you are likely to encounter in business and law contexts. We will break down complex legal jargon into simple, easy-to-understand language, providing clear definitions and practical examples for each term.

Mastering these terms will enhance your ability to comprehend legal documents, communicate effectively with legal professionals, and navigate the legal aspects of business with greater confidence. Let's begin with 60 essential legal vocabulary terms that are fundamental to understanding commercial law.

Legal Vocabulary

1. **Agreement:**
    - **Definition:** A mutual understanding between two or more parties about their rights and responsibilities.
    - **Example:** The partners signed an agreement to share profits equally.

2. **Arbitration:**
    - **Definition:** A method of resolving disputes outside of court where an arbitrator makes a binding decision.
    - **Example:** They chose arbitration to settle their contract dispute.

3. **Assets:**
    - **Definition:** Resources owned by a business or individual that have economic value.
    - **Example:** The company's assets include cash, equipment, and property.

4. **Breach:**
    - **Definition:** Failure to fulfill the terms of a contract.
    - **Example:** The supplier's late delivery constituted a breach of contract.

5. **Capital:**
    - **Definition:** Money or other assets used to start or grow a business.

- **Example**: She raised capital to launch her new startup.

6. **Claim**:
   - **Definition**: A demand for something due or believed to be due.
   - **Example**: The customer filed a claim for compensation after receiving faulty goods.

7. **Collateral**:
   - **Definition**: Property or assets pledged as security for a loan.
   - **Example**: He used his house as collateral for the business loan.

8. **Compliance**:
   - **Definition**: Adherence to laws, regulations, and company policies.
   - **Example**: The firm ensures compliance with all health and safety regulations.

9. **Contract**:
   - **Definition**: A legally binding agreement between two or more parties.
   - **Example**: They signed a contract to supply goods for one year.

10. **Creditor**:
    - **Definition**: A person or institution to whom money is owed.
    - **Example**: The business owes $10,000 to its creditors.

11. **Damages**:
    - **Definition**: Compensation for loss or injury.
    - **Example**: The court awarded damages for the breach of contract.

12. **Debtor**:
    - **Definition**: A person or entity that owes money.
    - **Example**: The debtor has six months to repay the loan.

13. **Defendant**:
    - **Definition**: The party against whom a lawsuit is filed.

- **Example**: The defendant denied all allegations of breach.

14. **Disclosure**:
    - **Definition**: The act of revealing information.
    - **Example**: Full financial disclosure is required during the audit.

15. **Equity**:
    - **Definition**: Ownership interest in a company.
    - **Example**: She holds 20% equity in the business.

16. **Fiduciary**:
    - **Definition**: A person who acts on behalf of another, managing their assets.
    - **Example**: The lawyer has a fiduciary duty to act in the best interests of the client.

17. **Franchise**:
    - **Definition**: A business model that allows individuals to operate a branch of a larger company.
    - **Example**: He purchased a fast-food franchise.

18. **Injunction**:
    - **Definition**: A court order requiring a party to do or refrain from doing a specific act.
    - **Example**: The court issued an injunction to stop the illegal activity.

19. **Intellectual Property**:
    - **Definition**: Creations of the mind, such as inventions, literary works, and trademarks.
    - **Example**: The patent is a form of intellectual property.

20. **Liability**:
    - **Definition**: Legal responsibility for one's actions or debts.
    - **Example**: The company faces liability for the faulty products.

21. **Litigation:**
    - **Definition:** The process of taking legal action.
    - **Example:** The dispute went into litigation.
22. **Mediation:**
    - **Definition:** A process in which a neutral third party helps resolve a dispute.
    - **Example:** Mediation helped the parties reach an amicable settlement.
23. **Merger:**
    - **Definition:** The combining of two or more entities into one.
    - **Example:** The merger of the two companies created a market leader.
24. **Negligence:**
    - **Definition:** Failure to take proper care in doing something.
    - **Example:** The doctor was sued for medical negligence.
25. **Offer:**
    - **Definition:** A proposal to enter into an agreement.
    - **Example:** She made an offer to purchase the property.
26. **Partnership:**
    - **Definition:** A business structure where two or more individuals share ownership and responsibilities.
    - **Example:** They formed a partnership to open a restaurant.
27. **Patent:**
    - **Definition:** Exclusive rights granted for an invention.
    - **Example:** He holds a patent for a new type of engine.
28. **Plaintiff:**
    - **Definition:** The party who initiates a lawsuit.
    - **Example:** The plaintiff seeks damages for breach of contract.

29. **Proprietor:**
    - **Definition:** An owner of a business.
    - **Example:** The sole proprietor manages the entire store.
30. **Proxy:**
    - **Definition:** Authority to act on behalf of another.
    - **Example:** He appointed a proxy to vote at the shareholders' meeting.
31. **Regulation:**
    - **Definition:** A rule or directive made and maintained by an authority.
    - **Example:** New environmental regulations were introduced last year.
32. **Remedy:**
    - **Definition:** A means of enforcing a right or compensating for a wrong.
    - **Example:** The court provided a remedy for the breach of contract.
33. **Revenue:**
    - **Definition:** Income generated from normal business operations.
    - **Example:** The company reported an increase in revenue this quarter.
34. **Securities:**
    - **Definition:** Financial instruments that represent an ownership position or creditor relationship.
    - **Example:** Stocks and bonds are types of securities.
35. **Settlement:**
    - **Definition:** An agreement reached between parties in a dispute.
    - **Example:** They reached a settlement before the case went to trial.
36. **Shareholder:**
    - **Definition:** An individual or entity that owns shares in a corporation.
    - **Example:** Shareholders receive dividends based on the company's profits.

37. **Statute:**
    - **Definition**: A written law passed by a legislative body.
    - **Example**: The new statute regulates online transactions.
38. **Subsidiary:**
    - **Definition**: A company controlled by another company.
    - **Example**: The corporation has several subsidiaries worldwide.
39. **Tort:**
    - **Definition**: A civil wrong that causes harm to another, leading to legal liability.
    - **Example**: The company was sued for the tort of negligence.
40. **Trademark:**
    - **Definition**: A symbol, word, or words legally registered for use as representing a company or product.
    - **Example**: The brand's trademark is instantly recognizable.
41. **Underwriter:**
    - **Definition**: A person or entity that assesses and assumes financial risk for a fee, often in insurance.
    - **Example**: The underwriter approved the insurance policy.
42. **Verdict:**
    - **Definition**: A decision on a disputed issue in a civil or criminal case.
    - **Example**: The jury returned a verdict of not guilty.
43. **Waiver:**
    - **Definition**: The voluntary relinquishment of a known right.
    - **Example**: He signed a waiver to give up his claim to the property.
44. **Warranty:**
    - **Definition**: A promise or guarantee provided by a seller regarding the condition of a product.

- **Example**: The car came with a five-year warranty.

45. **Whistleblower**:
    - **Definition**: A person who informs on a person or organization engaged in illicit activities.
    - **Example**: The whistleblower exposed the company's illegal practices.

46. **Will**:
    - **Definition**: A legal document expressing a person's wishes regarding the distribution of their property after death.
    - **Example**: The will specified the division of his estate among his children.

47. **Bankruptcy**:
    - **Definition**: A legal status for individuals or businesses that cannot repay their debts.
    - **Example**: The firm filed for bankruptcy after incurring heavy losses.

48. **Beneficiary**:
    - **Definition**: A person who benefits from a will, trust, or insurance policy.
    - **Example**: She was named as the sole beneficiary in her uncle's will.

49. **Confidentiality**:
    - **Definition**: The state of keeping or being kept secret or private.
    - **Example**: Lawyers are bound by confidentiality not to disclose client information.

50. **Conveyance**:
    - **Definition**: The act of transferring property from one party to another.
    - **Example**: The conveyance of the title was completed last week.

51. **Due Diligence**:
    - **Definition**: The investigation or audit of a potential investment.
    - **Example**: They performed due diligence before buying the company.

52. **Escrow:**
    - **Definition**: A financial arrangement where a third party holds and regulates payment of the funds required for two parties involved in a transaction.
    - **Example**: The money was held in escrow until all the conditions were met.

53. **Estoppel:**
    - **Definition**: A legal principle that prevents a party from arguing something contrary to a claim made or implied by their previous actions.
    - **Example**: The court ruled that estoppel applied, preventing the tenant from denying the lease terms.

54. **Force Majeure:**
    - **Definition**: A clause in contracts that frees parties from liability or obligation when an extraordinary event or circumstance beyond their control occurs.
    - **Example**: The contract included a force majeure clause to cover natural disasters.

55. **Foreclosure:**
    - **Definition**: The legal process by which a lender takes control of a property from a borrower who has defaulted on their mortgage.
    - **Example**: They faced foreclosure after failing to keep up with mortgage payments.

56. **Indemnity:**
    - **Definition**: Security or protection against a loss or other financial burden.
    - **Example**: The insurance policy provides indemnity against theft.

57. **Insolvency:**
    - **Definition**: The inability to pay debts when they are due.
    - **Example**: The company went into insolvency after a major client defaulted.

58. **Jurisdiction:**
    - **Definition**: The official power to make legal decisions and judgments.
    - **Example**: The case was transferred to a court with the proper jurisdiction.

59. **Lapse:**
    - **Definition**: The termination of a right or privilege due to the passage of time or failure to meet conditions.
    - **Example**: The insurance policy will lapse if the premium is not paid.

60. **Lien:**
    - **Definition**: A legal right or interest that a lender has in the borrower's property, granted until the debt is satisfied.
    - **Example**: The bank placed a lien on the property for the unpaid loan.

Conclusion

By familiarizing yourself with these key legal terms, you are taking an important step toward understanding and navigating the world of commercial law. These terms are not only foundational but also practical, offering a clearer perspective on legal documents and business operations. Continue to expand your legal vocabulary and deepen your understanding to become more proficient in the language of law and business.

SOLE PROPRIETORSHIP: WHAT IT IS, ITS ADVANTAGES AND DISADVANTAGES, AND HOW IT FUNCTIONS

Introduction

Welcome to our detailed exploration of the sole proprietorship, a fundamental concept in commercial law. This chapter aims to provide a comprehensive understanding of what a sole proprietorship is, its advantages and disadvantages, and how it functions in the business world. Using simple language and real-world examples, we will demystify this business structure to help you grasp its essentials easily.

Understanding Sole Proprietorship

A **sole proprietorship** is a type of business that is owned and operated by one individual. It is the simplest and most common form of business organization. In a sole proprietorship, there is no legal distinction between the owner and the business. This means that the owner is personally responsible for all aspects of the business, including its liabilities and debts.

Key Characteristics:

- **Single Ownership**: Only one person owns the business.
- **Full Control**: The owner makes all decisions and manages the business independently.
- **Personal Liability**: The owner is personally liable for all business obligations.
- **Simple Taxation**: Business income is taxed on the owner's personal tax return.

Advantages of a Sole Proprietorship

1. **Ease of Formation**: Setting up a sole proprietorship is straightforward. There are few legal formalities, and the initial costs are generally low.
    - **Example**: Jane decides to open a bakery called "Jane's Bakeshop." She does not need to register her business as a separate legal entity and can start operations quickly after obtaining necessary permits.
2. **Complete Control**: The owner has the autonomy to make all decisions related to the business. This can lead to quick decision-making and flexible operations.

- **Example**: David runs a photography business. He can decide on pricing, marketing strategies, and business hours without needing approval from others.
3. **Profit Retention**: The owner keeps all profits generated by the business. There is no requirement to share profits with partners or shareholders.
    - **Example**: Lisa, a freelance graphic designer, earns all the income from her projects, which she can reinvest in her business or use for personal expenses.
4. **Simple Taxation**: Business profits are reported on the owner's personal income tax return, which can simplify tax preparation and potentially lower tax obligations.
    - **Example**: Robert, who runs a small landscaping business, reports his business income on his individual tax return, avoiding the need to file separate business taxes.
5. **Less Regulatory Burden**: Sole proprietorships typically face fewer regulatory requirements compared to corporations or partnerships.
    - **Example**: Maria operates a home-based childcare service. She does not need to comply with the extensive regulations that larger daycare centers must follow.

Disadvantages of a Sole Proprietorship

1. **Unlimited Liability**: The owner is personally liable for all business debts and obligations. Personal assets can be used to settle business liabilities.
    - **Example**: If John's plumbing business incurs debt, creditors can pursue John's personal assets, such as his home or car, to recover the owed amount.
2. **Limited Capital**: Raising funds can be challenging, as sole proprietorships rely mainly on the owner's personal finances and may find it difficult to secure loans.
    - **Example**: Emma wants to expand her online clothing store but struggles to obtain a bank loan because her business lacks collateral.

3. **Lack of Continuity**: The business does not have a separate legal existence from the owner. Therefore, it may cease to exist if the owner retires, becomes incapacitated, or dies.
    - **Example**: When Tom, who runs a car repair shop, decides to retire, the business operations halt unless he transfers ownership or sells the business.
4. **Limited Expertise**: A sole proprietor may lack the diverse skills needed to handle all aspects of the business, such as marketing, finance, and legal issues.
    - **Example**: Rachel is an excellent chef but struggles with accounting and marketing for her catering business, which limits its growth potential.
5. **Difficulties in Attracting Talent**: It can be challenging to attract skilled employees or partners, as the business is seen as less stable compared to larger entities.
    - **Example**: Mark finds it hard to hire experienced staff for his tech support business, as candidates prefer the job security offered by larger companies.

Practical Examples

Example 1: High Tech Consulting Krishna is an IT professional who decides to start his own computer consulting business, "High Tech Consulting." He chooses to operate as a sole proprietorship because it allows him to have full control over his business decisions and keep all profits. However, Krishna must also consider that he will be personally liable for any debts or legal issues that arise in his business.

Example 2: Sarah's Sweets Sarah loves baking and wants to start a bakery, "Sarah's Sweets." She decides on a sole proprietorship because it's easy to set up and requires minimal paperwork. Sarah can manage her business flexibly and keep all earnings. However, she must be aware that if the bakery faces financial trouble, she will be personally responsible for the debts.

Example 3: Emily's Photography Emily is a passionate photographer who opens "Emily's Photography" as a sole proprietorship. She enjoys the freedom to make all business decisions and appreciates the direct tax benefits. Nevertheless, Emily knows that any liabilities or debts from her photography business are her personal responsibility.

Conclusion

A sole proprietorship is an attractive option for individuals looking to start a small business due to its simplicity, ease of formation, and full control over business operations. However, it comes with significant risks, particularly regarding personal liability and capital limitations. Understanding these factors is crucial for anyone considering a sole proprietorship, as it helps them make informed decisions about their business's future.

A HYPOTHETICAL CONVERSATION BETWEEN A LAWYER AND A CLIENT WHO IS SEEKING ADVICE ON CHOOSING THE BEST BUSINESS STRUCTURE

Introduction

Understanding how to navigate the complexities of business setup is crucial for new entrepreneurs. In this chapter, we will present a hypothetical conversation between a lawyer and a client who is seeking advice on choosing the best business structure. We will then analyze the conversation, breaking down the key points and providing practical insights to help you understand the process of setting up a business. This guide is written in simple English to be accessible for beginners.

The Conversation

Context: This conversation is between a lawyer and a client who wants to start a business but is unsure which business structure to choose. The discussion highlights the considerations involved in selecting the most appropriate type of business entity.

LAWYER: Good afternoon. How can I assist you today?

CLIENT: Good afternoon. I'm planning to start a new business and need some guidance on the best type of business structure to use.

LAWYER: Certainly. Can you tell me a bit more about your business idea?

CLIENT: I want to open a small boutique selling handmade jewelry. I've been making jewelry as a hobby for years, and now I'd like to turn it into a business.

LAWYER: That sounds exciting! Will you be running the business by yourself, or do you plan to have partners or employees?

CLIENT: I'll be running it on my own for now. I might hire an assistant later if the business grows.

LAWYER: Understood. How much money do you plan to invest in starting this business? Do you need any loans or financing?

CLIENT: I've saved up enough to cover the initial costs like inventory and setting up the store. I'm not planning to take out any loans at this time.

LAWYER: Great. Do you have a specific location in mind for your boutique, or will you be operating it online?

CLIENT: I've found a small space downtown that's perfect for a boutique. I'll start with a physical store and might expand online later.

LAWYER: It seems like you have a clear plan. Given that you'll be operating alone and have the necessary capital, a sole proprietorship could be a suitable option for you. It's simple to set up and gives you full control over your business.

CLIENT: That sounds good. Are there any risks I should be aware of with a sole proprietorship?

LAWYER: Yes, as a sole proprietor, you will be personally liable for all business debts and obligations. This means your personal assets could be at risk if the business faces financial difficulties or legal issues.

CLIENT: I see. What other options do I have?

LAWYER: Another option could be a limited liability company (LLC). It provides more protection for your personal assets but involves more paperwork and costs to set up and maintain.

CLIENT: I'm interested in the LLC. Can you tell me more about it?

LAWYER: An LLC combines the benefits of a sole proprietorship and a corporation. It offers limited liability protection, meaning your personal assets are generally protected from business debts. However, it requires registration with the state and ongoing compliance with legal requirements.

CLIENT: That sounds promising. I think I'll consider the LLC. Thank you for your advice!

LAWYER: You're welcome. I'm glad to help. Feel free to contact me if you need assistance with setting up your business.

Detailed Breakdown

1. **Business Idea and Scope:**
    - **Explanation**: The client is interested in opening a boutique selling handmade jewelry. This indicates a small-scale business that will start with a physical storefront and possibly expand online in the future.

- **Example**: Imagine Laura, who loves crafting handmade candles and decides to open a shop. She plans to manage the business herself, similar to the client's boutique idea.

2. **Ownership and Control**:
    - **Explanation**: The client will run the business alone, which means they will have full control over business decisions and operations without the need to share responsibilities or profits with partners.
    - **Example**: Jake, who operates a solo graphic design service, enjoys making all decisions himself, which is similar to the client's plan for their boutique.

3. **Capital Requirements**:
    - **Explanation**: The client has sufficient savings to cover startup costs and does not plan to seek external financing. This indicates a lower-risk venture in terms of financial investment.
    - **Example**: Maria starts a mobile pet grooming business with her own savings, covering the cost of equipment and a van, similar to how the client is financing their boutique.

4. **Business Location**:
    - **Explanation**: The client plans to open a physical store in a downtown location, which requires considerations such as rental costs, local regulations, and potential foot traffic.
    - **Example**: Chris wants to open a coffee shop in a busy area of town, considering factors like rent and customer access, much like the client's boutique location.

5. **Recommendation for Sole Proprietorship**:
    - **Explanation**: Given the simplicity and control desired, the lawyer recommends a sole proprietorship. This structure is easy to establish, involves minimal costs, and allows the owner to make all business decisions.
    - **Example**: Jane, running a small baking business from home, benefits from the simplicity and direct control offered by a sole proprietorship, just as the lawyer suggested for the client.

6. **Risks of Sole Proprietorship**:
   - **Explanation**: The main risk is unlimited personal liability. The owner is personally responsible for all business debts and legal obligations, which can endanger personal assets if the business fails.
   - **Example**: Emily, who operates a photography business, understands that her personal assets are at risk if her business encounters financial problems, highlighting the same concern mentioned to the client.

7. **Exploring LLC Option**:
   - **Explanation**: The lawyer introduces the LLC as an alternative that provides liability protection while still offering the simplicity of a sole proprietorship. This involves more setup and ongoing compliance but can protect personal assets.
   - **Example**: Alex, considering a consulting business, opts for an LLC to protect his personal savings and home from business liabilities, similar to the client's consideration of this option.

8. **Client's Decision**:
   - **Explanation**: The client expresses interest in the LLC for its liability protection and will consider this structure for setting up their business.
   - **Example**: Sarah, deciding on a business structure for her interior design firm, chooses an LLC for the added protection and flexibility, akin to the client's decision to explore this option further.

Practical Insights

Listening to Professional Advice:

- **Importance**: Seeking professional advice helps to understand the implications of different business structures and to choose the one that best aligns with personal goals and circumstances.
- **Example**: Mark, planning to start a small law practice, consults with a lawyer to understand the best structure for his needs, similar to how the client benefited from the lawyer's advice.

Evaluating Business Needs:

- **Key Considerations**: Understanding the business scope, capital requirements, and personal liability helps in selecting the right business structure. Factors like control, simplicity, and potential growth should be taken into account.
- **Example**: Lisa, starting an online fashion store, evaluates her needs and decides on a sole proprietorship due to its simplicity and ease of setup, much like the initial recommendation given to the client.

Understanding Liability:

- **Implications**: Choosing a business structure involves considering personal liability. A sole proprietorship exposes personal assets to business risks, while an LLC offers more protection.
- **Example**: John, opening a small construction business, decides on an LLC to shield his personal assets from business risks, reflecting the client's interest in the LLC for liability protection.

Conclusion

Choosing the right business structure is a critical step for any entrepreneur. As illustrated in this chapter, seeking professional advice and carefully evaluating business needs can lead to an informed decision that balances simplicity, control, and liability protection. Whether you opt for a sole proprietorship or consider the benefits of an LLC, understanding these concepts will help you establish a solid foundation for your business.

A CONVERSATION BETWEEN A LAWYER AND A CLIENT, FOCUSING ON THE BENEFITS AND DRAWBACKS OF SETTING UP A BUSINESS AS A SOLE PROPRIETOR

Introduction

Welcome to this comprehensive guide on understanding the advantages and disadvantages of sole proprietorships. In this chapter, we will present a conversation between a lawyer and a client, focusing on the benefits and drawbacks of setting up a business as a sole proprietor. We will analyze the dialogue in simple English to ensure it is accessible for beginners, providing clear explanations and practical examples to illustrate each point.

The Conversation

Context: This conversation takes place between a lawyer and a client who is considering starting a business as a sole proprietorship. The discussion highlights the key advantages and disadvantages of this business structure.

LAWYER: Good morning. How can I assist you today?

CLIENT: Good morning. I'm thinking about starting a business and I've heard that a sole proprietorship might be a good option. Can you tell me more about the pros and cons?

LAWYER: Of course. Sole proprietorships are quite popular, especially for small businesses. Let's start with the advantages. Firstly, a sole proprietorship is very easy to set up. There's minimal paperwork involved, and you don't need to register your business as a separate legal entity.

CLIENT: That sounds convenient. What about control over the business?

LAWYER: As a sole proprietor, you have complete control over all business decisions. This means you can manage your business the way you see fit without having to consult with partners or shareholders.

CLIENT: That's great. Are there any financial benefits?

LAWYER: Yes, there are. You get to keep all the profits from your business, and there's no need to share them with anyone else. Additionally, the tax process is simpler since business income is reported on your personal tax return.

CLIENT: That sounds like a lot of positives. Are there any downsides?

LAWYER: There are a few significant drawbacks to consider. The most important one is liability. As a sole proprietor, you are personally liable for all the debts and obligations of your business. This means that if your business incurs debt or faces legal action, your personal assets could be at risk.

CLIENT: That's a bit concerning. What about raising capital for the business?

LAWYER: It can be challenging. Sole proprietorships often find it harder to secure loans because they are seen as higher risk by lenders. You might need to rely on personal savings or assets to finance your business.

CLIENT: I see. Are there any other disadvantages I should be aware of?

LAWYER: Another issue is continuity. The business doesn't have a separate legal existence from you, so if something happens to you, the business might not survive. This can make it difficult to sell or pass on the business.

CLIENT: Thank you for explaining all this. It's a lot to think about, but I appreciate the clarity.

LAWYER: You're welcome. I'm glad I could help. Feel free to reach out if you have any more questions or need further assistance.

Detailed Breakdown

1. **Ease of Formation**:
    - **Explanation**: Setting up a sole proprietorship is straightforward. It requires minimal legal formalities, making it an accessible option for new business owners.
    - **Example**: Sarah decides to start a home-based bakery. She fills out a simple form to register her business name and begins operations without needing extensive legal paperwork.
2. **Complete Control**:

- **Explanation**: Sole proprietors have full authority over their business. They can make decisions quickly and adjust their operations as needed without seeking approval from others.
- **Example**: John runs a photography business and has the freedom to set his rates, choose his clients, and decide how to market his services, giving him flexibility and agility in managing his business.

3. **Profit Retention**:
    - **Explanation**: The owner retains all profits generated by the business, which can be reinvested into the business or used for personal purposes.
    - **Example**: Maria, who runs a freelance graphic design service, keeps all the earnings from her projects, which she can use to expand her business or save for personal goals.

4. **Simple Taxation**:
    - **Explanation**: Business income is reported on the owner's personal tax return, simplifying the tax process and potentially reducing tax obligations.
    - **Example**: Emily operates a small consulting firm and reports her business earnings on her individual tax return, making tax filing straightforward and avoiding the complexities of corporate taxes.

5. **Unlimited Liability**:
    - **Explanation**: The owner is personally responsible for all business debts and liabilities, which means personal assets can be used to satisfy business obligations.
    - **Example**: If Jake's carpentry business faces a lawsuit for faulty work, he might have to use his personal savings or property to pay the settlement, highlighting the risk of personal financial exposure.

6. **Challenges in Raising Capital**:
    - **Explanation**: Sole proprietorships may struggle to secure loans or attract investors due to perceived higher risk, often relying on personal funds for business financing.

- **Example**: Rachel wants to expand her tutoring service but finds it difficult to obtain a business loan without collateral, limiting her growth potential.

7. **Lack of Continuity**:
    - **Explanation**: The business is tied directly to the owner, so if the owner retires, passes away, or becomes incapacitated, the business may cease to exist or be difficult to transfer.
    - **Example**: When Tom, who runs a local bookstore, decides to retire, he faces challenges in selling the business because potential buyers are concerned about its reliance on his personal involvement.

Practical Insights

Evaluating the Benefits:

- **Why It's Important**: Understanding the advantages of sole proprietorships can help you decide if this structure aligns with your business goals, especially if you seek simplicity, full control, and easy setup.
- **Example**: Lisa, starting a personal fitness training business, values the ease of setup and direct control a sole proprietorship offers, making it the ideal choice for her.

Assessing the Risks:

- **Key Considerations**: Awareness of the risks, such as unlimited liability and difficulties in raising capital, is crucial for making informed decisions and preparing for potential challenges.
- **Example**: Alex, planning to open a small online store, weighs the risks of personal liability against the benefits of ease of setup, helping him make a balanced decision about his business structure.

Planning for Continuity:

- **Implications**: Considering how to ensure the business can continue without your direct involvement can help protect your investment and provide peace of mind.
- **Example**: Michael, running a sole proprietorship for his consulting business, sets up a contingency plan to ensure his clients are taken care of if he is unable to continue working.

Conclusion

Sole proprietorships offer a straightforward and flexible way to start a business, with the benefits of ease of setup, complete control, and simple taxation. However, they also come with significant risks, including unlimited liability and challenges in raising capital. By understanding these advantages and disadvantages, you can make an informed decision about whether a sole proprietorship is the right structure for your business. Listening to professional advice and carefully considering your personal circumstances and business goals will help you navigate the complexities of starting and managing a business successfully.

EXPLORE SOME CRITICAL QUESTIONS TO CONSIDER WHEN CHOOSING A BUSINESS STRUCTURE AND MANAGING LEGAL ASPECTS OF YOUR BUSINESS

Introduction

When starting a business, it's essential to ask yourself the right questions to make informed decisions. In this chapter, we will explore some critical questions to consider when choosing a business structure and managing legal aspects of your business. Using simple language, we will provide a comprehensive guide to help beginners think through these questions, with practical examples to illustrate each point.

Key Questions to Consider

Choosing the right business structure and understanding the legal implications of your business decisions can be complex. Here are some important questions to think about, along with detailed explanations and examples to help you navigate the decision-making process.

---

1. What are the advantages of a sole proprietorship?

Understanding the benefits of a sole proprietorship can help you decide if it's the right choice for your business. Here are three key advantages to consider:

- **Ease of Formation**: Setting up a sole proprietorship is straightforward, with minimal paperwork and costs involved.
    - **Example**: Jane wants to start a home-based bakery. She can simply register her business name and begin operations without complex legal procedures.
- **Complete Control**: As the sole owner, you have full control over all business decisions, allowing for quick and flexible management.
    - **Example**: David runs a freelance photography business and has the freedom to set his own rates and choose his clients without needing approval from others.
- **Direct Profits**: You keep all profits generated by the business, providing a direct financial benefit.

- o **Example**: Emma, who offers gardening services, earns all the income from her work, which she can reinvest into her business or use for personal expenses.

2. Why might another business structure be better than a sole proprietorship?

While sole proprietorships have many advantages, other structures might offer benefits that better suit your needs. Consider these three potential disadvantages of a sole proprietorship:

- **Unlimited Liability**: The owner is personally liable for all business debts, which means personal assets can be used to settle business obligations.
    - o **Example**: If John's plumbing business incurs debt, his personal savings and property could be at risk if the business fails to repay its loans.
- **Difficulty in Raising Capital**: Sole proprietorships may struggle to secure loans or attract investors, as they are often seen as higher risk.
    - o **Example**: Sarah wants to expand her home-based tutoring service but finds it challenging to obtain a bank loan without collateral.
- **Lack of Continuity**: The business is directly tied to the owner, so if the owner retires, becomes incapacitated, or passes away, the business may cease to exist.
    - o **Example**: Michael's local bookstore faces closure when he decides to retire, as it is difficult to transfer or sell the business without his continued involvement.

3. What skills might be necessary for your business?

Identifying the skills required to run your business effectively is crucial for success. Here are three key areas to consider:

- **Financial Management**: Understanding how to manage finances, including budgeting, accounting, and securing funding, is essential.
    - o **Example**: Laura, who runs a small catering business, must keep track of expenses, manage cash flow, and plan for future financial needs.
- **Marketing and Sales**: Effective marketing and sales skills are necessary to attract customers and grow your business.
    - o **Example**: Alex, a freelance web designer, uses social media and online advertising to promote his services and attract new clients.

- **Customer Service**: Providing excellent customer service helps build a loyal customer base and enhances your business reputation.
    - **Example**: Rachel, who owns a pet grooming service, ensures her clients are satisfied by providing personalized attention and addressing any concerns promptly.

4. Is there a problem with finance?

Evaluating potential financial challenges is important to ensure your business's stability and growth. Consider these three questions:

- **Do you have sufficient startup capital?**: Assess whether you have enough funds to cover initial costs, including equipment, supplies, and marketing.
    - **Example**: Mark, starting a tech repair service, needs to ensure he has enough money to purchase tools and software needed for his work.
- **Can you manage cash flow effectively?**: Maintaining a healthy cash flow is critical for meeting ongoing expenses and sustaining your business.
    - **Example**: Lisa, who operates a small boutique, tracks her income and expenses carefully to ensure she can pay rent, utilities, and inventory costs on time.
- **Are you able to secure funding if needed?**: Determine if you can access additional financing, such as loans or investments, to support business growth or handle unexpected expenses.
    - **Example**: Tom considers applying for a small business loan to expand his coffee shop but needs to ensure he meets the requirements and can repay the loan.

5. Would a partnership be a better choice than a sole proprietorship?

Forming a partnership can offer advantages over a sole proprietorship, especially if you plan to collaborate with others. Consider these three benefits:

- **Shared Responsibility**: Partners can share the workload and bring different skills and expertise to the business.
    - **Example**: Emma and Jake start a landscaping business together. Emma handles client relations, while Jake focuses on the technical work, combining their strengths for a successful venture.

- **Increased Capital**: Partners can pool their resources, making it easier to raise capital and invest in the business.
    - **Example**: Sarah and David partner to open a restaurant, combining their savings to cover startup costs and secure a prime location.
- **Risk Sharing**: Risks and liabilities are shared among partners, reducing the individual burden on each owner.
    - **Example**: Alex and Maria form a partnership for their event planning business. If the business faces financial difficulties, they share the responsibility for managing debts and obligations.

Practical Insights

Evaluating Business Structures:

- **Why It's Important**: Choosing the right business structure impacts your liability, tax obligations, and ability to raise capital. It's essential to consider all options carefully.
- **Example**: John, planning to start a delivery service, evaluates the benefits of a partnership over a sole proprietorship, ultimately deciding on a partnership to leverage shared resources and reduce personal liability.

Identifying Necessary Skills:

- **Key Considerations**: Understanding the skills required for your business helps you plan for training, hiring, or collaborating with others to fill skill gaps.
- **Example**: Lisa identifies a need for better financial management skills and decides to take a course in small business accounting to improve her abilities and manage her boutique more effectively.

Planning for Financial Challenges:

- **Implications**: Being prepared for financial challenges ensures your business can withstand fluctuations in income and unexpected expenses, maintaining stability and growth.
- **Example**: Mark creates a financial plan for his tech repair service, including strategies for managing cash flow and securing additional funding if needed, to support his business's long-term success.

Conclusion

Thinking through these key questions helps you make informed decisions about your business structure, required skills, and financial planning. By carefully considering the advantages and disadvantages of different business setups and being aware of potential challenges, you can establish a strong foundation for your business and navigate the complexities of commercial law with confidence.

A PARTNERSHIP: WHAT IT IS, ITS TYPES, ADVANTAGES, AND DISADVANTAGES

Introduction

Welcome to our comprehensive guide on partnerships in commercial law. In this chapter, we will explore what a partnership is, its types, advantages, and disadvantages, along with practical examples to help you understand this business structure. This guide uses simple language to ensure it is accessible for beginners and provides a detailed look into the workings of a partnership.

Understanding Partnerships

A **partnership** is a business structure where two or more individuals (partners) agree to share the profits, losses, and responsibilities of a business. Unlike a sole proprietorship, a partnership involves multiple owners who jointly manage and operate the business.

Key Characteristics:

- **Co-Ownership**: Partners share ownership and responsibilities.
- **Shared Decision-Making**: All partners are involved in the management of the business.
- **Profit and Loss Sharing**: Profits and losses are distributed among the partners based on their agreement.
- **Personal Liability**: Partners may have unlimited liability for business debts.

Types of Partnerships

1. **General Partnership**:
    - **Definition**: In a general partnership, all partners share equal responsibility for the business's management and liabilities.
    - **Example**: William and Sophie start a diet advice clinic called "Nutrition for Life." William manages finances, and Sophie provides diet consultations. Both share the profits and are equally liable for any business debts.

2. **Limited Partnership**:

- **Definition**: This type includes general partners who manage the business and are liable for its debts, and limited partners who invest money but have limited liability and do not participate in daily operations.
- **Example**: Alex and Maria start a real estate firm. Alex manages the business as a general partner, while Maria, a limited partner, provides capital but does not take part in daily management.

3. **Limited Liability Partnership (LLP)**:
    - **Definition**: In an LLP, all partners have limited liability, meaning they are not personally responsible for business debts. It combines elements of partnerships and corporations.
    - **Example**: John and Lisa start a law firm as an LLP, which protects their personal assets from business liabilities while allowing them to manage the business together.

Advantages of Partnerships

1. **Ease of Formation**:
    - **Explanation**: Partnerships are relatively simple and inexpensive to set up compared to corporations. They require minimal legal paperwork.
    - **Example**: Tom and Jerry decide to start a home renovation business. They form a general partnership by drafting a simple partnership agreement, which allows them to start their business quickly and with low costs.

2. **Diverse Skill Set**:
    - **Explanation**: Partners can bring different skills, experiences, and resources to the business, enhancing its potential for success.
    - **Example**: Emily and Jack start a marketing agency. Emily has expertise in digital marketing, while Jack excels in sales. Their combined skills help the agency grow rapidly by offering comprehensive services to clients.

3. **Shared Responsibility**:
    - **Explanation**: Partners share the workload, decision-making, and management responsibilities, which can reduce individual stress and workload.

- **Example**: Sarah and David run a café together. Sarah handles daily operations, and David manages supply orders. By dividing responsibilities, they efficiently manage the business and maintain work-life balance.

4. **Access to Capital**:
    - **Explanation**: Partnerships often find it easier to raise capital since multiple partners can contribute resources and potentially attract investors more effectively than a sole proprietor.
    - **Example**: Jane and Mike plan to open a gym. By pooling their savings and obtaining a small business loan, they are able to secure a larger space and purchase quality equipment, which attracts more clients.

5. **Flexibility in Management**:
    - **Explanation**: Partnerships offer flexibility in management and operations, allowing partners to adapt to changes and make quick decisions.
    - **Example**: Rachel and Tim start a tech startup. They frequently adjust their business model and strategies based on market feedback, leveraging their partnership's flexibility to stay competitive.

Disadvantages of Partnerships

1. **Unlimited Liability**:
    - **Explanation**: In a general partnership, partners are personally liable for all business debts and obligations. This means that personal assets can be at risk.
    - **Example**: If Alex's and Maria's real estate firm incurs significant debt, both partners could be held responsible for repaying the debt, risking their personal savings and assets.

2. **Potential for Conflicts**:
    - **Explanation**: Disagreements between partners can arise, particularly regarding business decisions, profit distribution, or roles and responsibilities.

- **Example**: John and Lisa, running a law firm, argue over the firm's expansion plans. Their conflict leads to tension and disrupts business operations until they resolve their differences through mediation.

3. **Limited Continuity**:
    - **Explanation**: The partnership may dissolve if a partner leaves, becomes incapacitated, or dies, potentially threatening the business's stability.
    - **Example**: When Mike, a partner in a gym business, decides to retire, the partnership agreement requires the gym to be sold or restructured, impacting its continuity and operations.

4. **Shared Profits**:
    - **Explanation**: Profits must be shared among partners, which may lead to dissatisfaction if partners feel their contributions are not equally rewarded.
    - **Example**: Sarah feels that she contributes more to the café's success than David but receives an equal share of profits, leading to resentment and discussions about adjusting the profit-sharing arrangement.

5. **Joint and Several Liability**:
    - **Explanation**: Each partner can be held responsible for the business's debts and obligations, regardless of who incurred them.
    - **Example**: If one partner in a landscaping business signs a large contract without the other's knowledge, both partners could be liable if the business fails to meet the contractual obligations.

Practical Examples

Example 1: Nutrition for Life William and Sophie start a diet advice clinic, "Nutrition for Life," as a general partnership. They each bring different skills to the table—William handles the finances, and Sophie provides dietary advice. They share profits equally, but they also share any losses and liabilities the business may incur.

Example 2: Green Thumb Landscaping John and David form a limited partnership for their landscaping business. John, the general partner, manages the business and takes on full liability, while David, the limited partner, contributes capital but is not involved in day-to-day operations. This setup allows them to combine their resources while protecting David's personal assets.

Example 3: Creative Solutions LLP Emma and Jack start a consulting firm, "Creative Solutions," as an LLP. Both partners share management responsibilities and have limited liability, protecting their personal assets from business debts. This structure helps them collaborate effectively while minimizing their financial risks.

Conclusion

Partnerships offer a flexible and collaborative business structure that can enhance a business's potential for success. By sharing responsibilities, skills, and resources, partners can build a stronger and more resilient business. However, it's important to be aware of the potential risks, such as unlimited liability and conflicts, and to plan accordingly to mitigate these challenges.

A CONVERSATION BETWEEN A LAWYER AND A CLIENT WHO IS CONSIDERING FORMING A PARTNERSHIP FOR THEIR NEW BUSINESS

Introduction

Starting a business partnership can provide several benefits, such as shared resources and responsibilities. In this chapter, we will present a conversation between a lawyer and a client who is considering forming a partnership for their new business. We will analyze the dialogue in simple English to ensure it is accessible for beginners, providing clear explanations and practical examples to illustrate each point. This will help you understand the key aspects of setting up a partnership and the legal considerations involved.

The Conversation

Context: This conversation is between a lawyer and a client who is seeking advice on forming a partnership for a new business. The discussion highlights important considerations and legal aspects of establishing a partnership.

LAWYER: Good afternoon. How can I help you today?

CLIENT: Good afternoon. I'm planning to start a business with my friend, and we're thinking about forming a partnership. I'd like some advice on how to go about it.

LAWYER: Certainly. Can you tell me more about the business you're planning to start?

CLIENT: We want to open a small café and bakery. My friend, Emily, is a great baker, and I'll handle the business operations.

LAWYER: That sounds like a solid plan. Will you both be equally involved in managing the business?

CLIENT: Yes, we plan to share the responsibilities equally. We'll both contribute to the initial investment and decision-making.

LAWYER: Excellent. Do you have an idea of how much capital you'll need to start the business and how you plan to raise it?

CLIENT: We've estimated about $50,000 to cover the rent, equipment, and initial supplies. We both have some savings and are considering a small business loan.

LAWYER: That's a good start. Given your shared responsibilities and financial contributions, a partnership seems like a suitable choice. Have you thought about the type of partnership you want to form?

CLIENT: Not really. What are our options?

LAWYER: You have a few options, such as a general partnership, where both partners share equal responsibility and liability, or a limited partnership, where one partner manages the business while the other provides capital but has limited liability.

CLIENT: We want to be equally involved in the business, so a general partnership sounds more appropriate for us.

LAWYER: In that case, you'll need to draft a partnership agreement to outline each partner's roles, responsibilities, and how profits and losses will be shared. This helps prevent future disputes.

CLIENT: That makes sense. Is setting up a partnership a complicated process?

LAWYER: Not usually. It involves creating a partnership agreement and registering your business. I can help you with the paperwork and ensure everything is set up correctly.

CLIENT: Thank you. We'll definitely need your help with the agreement. What should we include in it?

LAWYER: You should include details like each partner's capital contribution, roles and responsibilities, profit and loss sharing, and procedures for resolving disputes and handling the departure of a partner.

CLIENT: That's very helpful. We'll work on that and get back to you soon.

LAWYER: Great. I'm here to help you with any legal aspects as you set up your business. Good luck with your new venture!

Detailed Breakdown

1. **Business Idea and Scope**:
    - **Explanation**: The client plans to start a café and bakery with a friend, where they will share responsibilities and manage the business together.

- **Example**: Similar to how John and Lisa plan to open a shared office space business, the client and Emily will collaborate on managing the café and bakery, each bringing their expertise to the venture.

2. **Shared Responsibilities**:
   - **Explanation**: Both partners will be equally involved in the business, sharing decision-making and operational duties.
   - **Example**: Like Rachel and Tim, who run a tech startup together, each partner in the café and bakery will handle different aspects of the business, such as baking and business operations, to ensure smooth functioning.

3. **Capital Requirements**:
   - **Explanation**: The client and their partner have estimated the startup costs and plan to use their savings and potentially a loan to cover these expenses.
   - **Example**: Similar to how Tom and Jerry started their home renovation business with a clear budget and financial plan, the client and Emily will secure the necessary funds for their café and bakery.

4. **Types of Partnerships**:
   - **Explanation**: The lawyer explains the different types of partnerships, including general and limited partnerships, and helps the client decide on a general partnership based on their needs.
   - **Example**: Emma and Jack chose a general partnership for their consulting firm because they both wanted equal involvement in management and decision-making, which aligns with the client's preference for their café.

5. **Importance of a Partnership Agreement**:
   - **Explanation**: Drafting a partnership agreement is crucial for defining each partner's roles, responsibilities, and financial contributions, which helps prevent future conflicts.
   - **Example**: Sarah and David created a detailed partnership agreement for their café, specifying their roles and how they would handle profits, losses, and potential disputes, similar to the advice given to the client.

6. **Ease of Setting Up a Partnership:**
    - **Explanation:** Setting up a partnership involves drafting an agreement and registering the business, which is typically straightforward with the right legal assistance.
    - **Example:** Mark and Rachel quickly set up their tech repair partnership by drafting an agreement and registering their business, demonstrating that with proper guidance, forming a partnership can be simple and efficient.

Practical Insights

Evaluating the Business Structure:

- **Why It's Important:** Choosing the right business structure is essential for managing liabilities, sharing responsibilities, and ensuring smooth operations. A partnership can provide a balanced approach for businesses that require shared management and resources.
- **Example:** John and Lisa opted for a partnership for their shared office space business, allowing them to combine their resources and expertise effectively.

Planning for Financial Needs:

- **Key Considerations:** Understanding the financial requirements and planning for capital investment helps ensure the business has the necessary resources to start and grow. Partnerships allow for shared financial contributions, making it easier to raise funds.
- **Example:** Mark and Rachel pooled their savings and secured a small loan to cover startup expenses for their tech repair service, similar to how the client and Emily plan to finance their café and bakery.

Drafting a Partnership Agreement:

- **Implications:** A well-drafted partnership agreement clarifies each partner's roles, responsibilities, and profit-sharing arrangements, reducing the risk of conflicts and ensuring smooth operations.
- **Example:** Emma and Jack included detailed provisions in their partnership agreement for their consulting firm, ensuring clarity on each partner's duties and financial contributions, which helped prevent disputes.

Conclusion

Starting a partnership involves careful planning and consideration of each partner's roles, responsibilities, and financial contributions. By understanding the benefits and challenges of a partnership, you can make informed decisions that align with your business goals and ensure a successful collaboration. Listening to professional advice and drafting a clear partnership agreement are essential steps in setting up a solid and effective business partnership.

A CONVERSATION BETWEEN A LAWYER AND A CLIENT WHO HAS QUESTIONS ABOUT CREATING A PARTNERSHIP AGREEMENT FOR A NEW BUSINESS

Introduction

When forming a partnership, it is essential to understand the key components and implications of a partnership agreement. In this chapter, we will explore a conversation between a lawyer and a client who has questions about creating a partnership agreement for a new business. We will analyze the dialogue in simple English to ensure it is accessible for beginners, providing clear explanations and practical examples to illustrate each point. This guide will help you understand the importance of a partnership agreement and what it should include.

The Conversation

Context: The following conversation is between a lawyer and a client who is seeking advice on forming a partnership and creating a partnership agreement for a new business. The dialogue highlights important questions and considerations related to setting up a partnership agreement.

LAWYER: Good morning, Mr. Anderson. How can I assist you today?

CLIENT: Good morning, Ms. Carter. I'm planning to start a business with my friend, and we need some advice on forming a partnership. We have some questions about the partnership agreement.

LAWYER: Of course, I'd be happy to help. What kind of business are you planning to start?

CLIENT: We want to open a bookstore and coffee shop. My friend, Anna, is passionate about books, and I love coffee. We thought it would be a great combination.

LAWYER: That sounds like a wonderful idea. Will both of you be equally involved in running the business?

CLIENT: Yes, we plan to manage it together and share responsibilities equally. We'll both invest in the business and handle different aspects of its operations.

LAWYER: Excellent. A partnership could be a good choice for you. Have you thought about what you want to include in your partnership agreement?

CLIENT: Not really. What should we include in it?

LAWYER: You should include the roles and responsibilities of each partner, how profits and losses will be shared, how decisions will be made, and how to handle the departure of a partner.

CLIENT: That makes sense. Do we need to include anything about what happens if we disagree?

LAWYER: Yes, it's a good idea to include a dispute resolution process. This could involve mediation or arbitration to resolve conflicts without going to court.

CLIENT: OK. What about finances? How should we handle our investments and profits?

LAWYER: Your agreement should specify how much each partner will invest initially, how additional funds will be raised if needed, and how profits and losses will be divided.

CLIENT: What if one of us wants to leave the partnership? How do we handle that?

LAWYER: You should include a clause about the process for a partner to leave, such as how their share of the business will be valued and whether the remaining partner has the option to buy them out.

CLIENT: That's helpful. Is there anything else we need to consider?

LAWYER: Yes, you should also include provisions for how the partnership will be dissolved if you both decide to end the business. This ensures a clear plan for winding down operations and distributing assets.

CLIENT: Thank you for your advice. We'll need your help with drafting the agreement.

LAWYER: I'd be happy to help you with that. Let's schedule a time to draft your partnership agreement and ensure it covers all the necessary aspects.

CLIENT: Great. We'll get back to you soon to set up a meeting.

LAWYER: Excellent. I look forward to working with you and Anna on your new venture.

Detailed Breakdown

1. **Business Idea and Scope**:
   - **Explanation**: The client and their friend plan to start a bookstore and coffee shop together, where they will share management and operational responsibilities.
   - **Example**: Similar to how Sarah and David started a shared café, Mr. Anderson and Anna will manage their bookstore and coffee shop together, each focusing on different aspects of the business.

2. **Shared Responsibilities**:
   - **Explanation**: Both partners will be equally involved in the business, sharing investment, management, and decision-making responsibilities.
   - **Example**: Rachel and Tim, running a tech startup, divided their roles and responsibilities to ensure efficient management, just as Mr. Anderson and Anna will do for their bookstore and coffee shop.

3. **Importance of a Partnership Agreement**:
   - **Explanation**: The lawyer explains that a partnership agreement should outline roles, responsibilities, profit-sharing, decision-making processes, and how to handle a partner's departure.
   - **Example**: Alex and Maria created a partnership agreement for their boutique, specifying each partner's duties and how profits would be divided, which helped prevent conflicts and ensure clear expectations.

4. **Including Dispute Resolution**:
   - **Explanation**: Including a dispute resolution process in the agreement helps resolve conflicts without legal battles, which can be costly and time-consuming.
   - **Example**: John and Lisa included a mediation clause in their partnership agreement for their shared office space business to handle potential disagreements, similar to the advice given to Mr. Anderson.

5. **Handling Finances**:

- **Explanation**: The agreement should specify each partner's initial investment, how additional funds will be raised, and how profits and losses will be divided.
- **Example**: Mark and Rachel outlined their financial contributions and profit-sharing plan in their tech repair service's partnership agreement, ensuring clear and fair financial management.

6. **Managing Partner Departure**:
    - **Explanation**: The agreement should include a clause on how to handle the departure of a partner, such as valuing their share and providing an option for the remaining partner to buy them out.
    - **Example**: Emma and Jack added a buyout clause to their partnership agreement for their consulting firm, which provided a clear process if one of them decided to leave the business.

7. **Dissolution of the Partnership**:
    - **Explanation**: Including provisions for dissolving the partnership ensures a clear plan for winding down the business and distributing assets if both partners decide to end the business.
    - **Example**: Sarah and David included a dissolution clause in their café partnership agreement, outlining how they would handle closing the business and dividing assets if they decided to end the partnership.

Practical Insights

Evaluating the Need for a Partnership Agreement:

- **Why It's Important**: A partnership agreement provides clarity on roles, responsibilities, and financial contributions, reducing the risk of conflicts and ensuring smooth operations.
- **Example**: John and Lisa, setting up a shared office space business, drafted a partnership agreement to outline their contributions and how they would manage the business, preventing potential disagreements and legal issues.

Planning for Financial and Legal Considerations:

- **Key Considerations**: Understanding the financial and legal responsibilities of a partnership helps in planning for capital investment, managing liabilities, and ensuring compliance with tax regulations.

- **Example**: Mark and Rachel, starting a tech repair service, planned for their financial needs and legal responsibilities by securing a loan and drafting a clear agreement on their roles and profit sharing.

Preparing for Potential Issues:

- **Implications**: Being aware of potential challenges, such as disagreements and funding difficulties, helps in preparing strategies to address these issues and maintain a healthy business relationship.
- **Example**: Sarah and David, running a café, prepared for potential conflicts by setting up regular meetings to discuss their business plans and address any issues promptly, ensuring a collaborative approach to managing their business.

Conclusion

Understanding the key aspects of a partnership agreement is crucial for setting up a successful partnership. By addressing important questions and legal considerations, you can ensure a clear and fair arrangement with your business partner, reducing the risk of conflicts and ensuring smooth operations. Listening to professional advice and preparing a detailed partnership agreement are essential steps in establishing a solid foundation for your business.

COMMON LEGAL TERMS USED IN THE CONTEXT OF PARTNERSHIPS: PART TWO

Introduction

Welcome to the second part of our comprehensive guide on legal vocabulary related to partnerships in commercial law. In this chapter, we will introduce 60 essential legal terms that are commonly used in the context of partnerships. Each term will be explained in simple English, with practical examples to help you understand how they are used in real-world situations. This guide aims to provide beginners with a solid foundation in legal vocabulary, making it easier for them to navigate and comprehend partnership agreements and other legal documents.

Legal Vocabulary

1. **Acquisition**:
   - **Definition**: The process of obtaining ownership or control of a company or asset.
   - **Example**: The partnership decided on the acquisition of a smaller competitor to expand their market presence.

2. **Agreement**:
   - **Definition**: A mutual understanding between parties about their rights and responsibilities.
   - **Example**: The partners signed an agreement outlining their roles in the new business venture.

3. **Arbitration**:
   - **Definition**: A method of resolving disputes outside of court by a neutral third party.
   - **Example**: The partners agreed to use arbitration to settle any disagreements regarding the business.

4. **Assets**:
   - **Definition**: Resources owned by a business that have economic value.
   - **Example**: The partnership's assets included real estate, inventory, and equipment.

5. **Breach:**
    - **Definition:** Failure to fulfill the terms of a contract.
    - **Example:** One partner's failure to invest agreed funds was considered a breach of the partnership agreement.
6. **Capital:**
    - **Definition:** Money or other assets used to start and grow a business.
    - **Example:** Each partner contributed capital to fund the initial operations of the partnership.
7. **Confidentiality:**
    - **Definition:** The obligation to keep certain information private.
    - **Example:** The partners signed a confidentiality agreement to protect the business's trade secrets.
8. **Conflict of Interest:**
    - **Definition:** A situation where a person's personal interests could interfere with their professional duties.
    - **Example:** A partner was required to disclose any potential conflicts of interest to avoid compromising the partnership.
9. **Consideration:**
    - **Definition:** Something of value exchanged between parties in a contract.
    - **Example:** The partnership agreement specified the consideration each partner would receive for their contributions.
10. **Contribution:**
    - **Definition:** The act of providing capital or resources to a partnership.
    - **Example:** Each partner made an equal contribution of funds to start the business.
11. **Dissolution:**
    - **Definition:** The process of ending a partnership or business.

- **Example**: The partnership agreement included provisions for dissolution if the business ceased operations.

12. **Dispute Resolution**:
    - **Definition**: Methods for resolving disagreements between parties.
    - **Example**: The partnership agreement outlined dispute resolution procedures such as mediation and arbitration.

13. **Dividend**:
    - **Definition**: A distribution of profits to partners or shareholders.
    - **Example**: At the end of the fiscal year, the partners received a dividend based on the profits earned.

14. **Due Diligence**:
    - **Definition**: The investigation of a business before entering into a contract.
    - **Example**: The partners conducted due diligence before acquiring a new business asset.

15. **Equity**:
    - **Definition**: Ownership interest in a business.
    - **Example**: Each partner's equity in the business was determined by their initial investment.

16. **Fiduciary Duty**:
    - **Definition**: The legal obligation to act in the best interest of another party.
    - **Example**: The partners had a fiduciary duty to act in the best interests of the business and each other.

17. **Indemnity**:
    - **Definition**: Compensation for damage or loss.
    - **Example**: The partnership agreement included an indemnity clause to cover potential losses.

18. **Insolvency**:

- **Definition**: The inability to pay debts when they are due.
- **Example**: The partners faced insolvency after the business failed to generate sufficient revenue.

19. **Intellectual Property**:
    - **Definition**: Creations of the mind, such as inventions and trademarks.
    - **Example**: The partnership's intellectual property included several patents and registered trademarks.

20. **Joint Liability**:
    - **Definition**: Shared legal responsibility among partners for business debts.
    - **Example**: The partners had joint liability for all debts incurred by the business.

21. **Limited Liability**:
    - **Definition**: Liability limited to the amount invested in the partnership.
    - **Example**: The limited partners had limited liability and were not personally responsible for business debts.

22. **Mediation**:
    - **Definition**: A process in which a neutral third party helps resolve disputes.
    - **Example**: The partners used mediation to resolve a disagreement over profit distribution.

23. **Non-Disclosure Agreement (NDA)**:
    - **Definition**: A contract that restricts sharing confidential information.
    - **Example**: The partners signed an NDA to protect sensitive business information.

24. **Operating Agreement**:
    - **Definition**: A document outlining the management and operation of a partnership.

- **Example**: The partnership's operating agreement detailed each partner's role and decision-making authority.

25. **Partnership**:
    - **Definition**: A business structure where two or more individuals share ownership and responsibilities.
    - **Example**: John and Lisa formed a partnership to open a shared office space business.

26. **Partnership Agreement**:
    - **Definition**: A contract that outlines the terms of a partnership.
    - **Example**: The partners drafted a partnership agreement specifying their contributions and profit-sharing arrangements.

27. **Profit Sharing**:
    - **Definition**: The distribution of profits among partners.
    - **Example**: The partnership agreement included a profit-sharing plan based on each partner's investment.

28. **Quorum**:
    - **Definition**: The minimum number of partners needed to conduct business.
    - **Example**: The partnership agreement required a quorum of three partners for decision-making.

29. **Registration**:
    - **Definition**: The process of legally recording a business with authorities.
    - **Example**: The partnership completed its registration with the local government to operate legally.

30. **Resolution**:
    - **Definition**: A formal decision made by partners.
    - **Example**: The partners passed a resolution to expand the business to a new location.

31. **Retained Earnings**:

- Definition: Profits that are reinvested in the business rather than distributed to partners.
- Example: The partners decided to use retained earnings to fund the purchase of new equipment.

32. **Share**:
    - **Definition**: A unit of ownership in a business.
    - **Example**: Each partner's share in the partnership was determined by their initial investment.

33. **Shareholder**:
    - **Definition**: An individual or entity that owns shares in a business.
    - **Example**: The partners decided to bring in additional shareholders to raise capital.

34. **Solvency**:
    - **Definition**: The ability to meet long-term financial obligations.
    - **Example**: The partners ensured the business's solvency by maintaining a healthy cash flow.

35. **Tax Liability**:
    - **Definition**: The amount of tax owed by a business or individual.
    - **Example**: The partnership's tax liability was shared among the partners based on their profit shares.

36. **Termination Clause**:
    - **Definition**: A provision outlining how a partnership can be ended.
    - **Example**: The partnership agreement included a termination clause specifying the process for dissolving the business.

37. **Trade Name**:
    - **Definition**: The name under which a business operates.
    - **Example**: The partners registered the trade name "Books & Brews" for their bookstore and coffee shop.

38. **Underwriting:**
    - **Definition**: The process of assessing and assuming risk for a fee.
    - **Example**: The partners worked with an insurance company for the underwriting of their business's insurance policy.

39. **Valuation:**
    - **Definition**: The process of determining the value of a business or asset.
    - **Example**: The partners conducted a valuation of their business to attract potential investors.

40. **Vesting:**
    - **Definition**: The process by which a partner earns the right to benefits or ownership over time.
    - **Example**: The partnership agreement included a vesting schedule for each partner's ownership shares.

41. **Waiver:**
    - **Definition**: The voluntary relinquishment of a right or claim.
    - **Example**: The partners signed a waiver to forgo any claims against each other for previous business disputes.

42. **Working Capital:**
    - **Definition**: The funds available for the day-to-day operations of a business.
    - **Example**: The partners ensured sufficient working capital to cover operating expenses and unexpected costs.

43. **Yield:**
    - **Definition**: The return on an investment.
    - **Example**: The partnership's yield on their investment in new technology exceeded expectations.

44. **Zoning Laws:**
    - **Definition**: Regulations governing the use of land and buildings.

- **Example**: The partners ensured their new business location complied with local zoning laws.

45. **Addendum**:
    - **Definition**: A document added to a contract to include additional terms or information.
    - **Example**: The partners added an addendum to their agreement to cover the new responsibilities of a third partner.

46. **Amendment**:
    - **Definition**: A change or addition to a legal document.
    - **Example**: The partnership agreement was updated with an amendment to reflect changes in profit-sharing.

47. **Arbitration Clause**:
    - **Definition**: A section in a contract that requires disputes to be resolved through arbitration.
    - **Example**: The partnership agreement included an arbitration clause to handle any legal disputes.

48. **Assignment**:
    - **Definition**: The transfer of rights or property to another party.
    - **Example**: The partners agreed to the assignment of certain business tasks to external consultants.

49. **Breach of Fiduciary Duty**:
    - **Definition**: A failure to act in the best interests of another party, violating trust.
    - **Example**: One partner's misuse of company funds was considered a breach of fiduciary duty.

50. **Capital Contribution**:
    - **Definition**: The funds or assets that a partner provides to a business.
    - **Example**: Each partner's capital contribution was documented in the partnership agreement.

51. **Contingency Plan:**
    - **Definition:** A strategy for dealing with unexpected events or emergencies.
    - **Example:** The partners developed a contingency plan for potential business disruptions.
52. **Domicile:**
    - **Definition:** The legal residence or principal place of business.
    - **Example:** The partnership's domicile was listed as the primary office location in the legal documents.
53. **Escrow:**
    - **Definition:** A financial arrangement where a third party holds funds or assets until conditions are met.
    - **Example:** The partners used escrow to manage the transfer of ownership shares.
54. **Good Faith:**
    - **Definition:** Honesty and fairness in business dealings.
    - **Example:** The partners agreed to act in good faith in all business transactions.
55. **Indemnification:**
    - **Definition:** Protection against loss or damage.
    - **Example:** The partnership agreement included indemnification clauses to protect partners from certain liabilities.
56. **Jurisdiction:**
    - **Definition:** The authority to make legal decisions and judgments.
    - **Example:** The partnership's legal disputes would be resolved in the jurisdiction where the business is registered.
57. **Lien:**
    - **Definition:** A legal claim on assets for the payment of a debt.

- **Example**: The partnership faced a lien on their property due to an unpaid loan.

58. **Non-Compete Clause**:
    - **Definition**: A provision preventing partners from engaging in competing businesses.
    - **Example**: The partners included a non-compete clause in their agreement to protect the business from internal competition.

59. **Power of Attorney**:
    - **Definition**: Legal authority to act on behalf of another person.
    - **Example**: One partner granted the other power of attorney to manage business affairs during their absence.

60. **Retainer**:
    - **Definition**: An advance payment for professional services.
    - **Example**: The partnership paid a retainer to their lawyer for ongoing legal services.

Practical Examples

Example 1: Books & Brews John and Lisa formed a partnership to open a bookstore and coffee shop called "Books & Brews." They drafted a partnership agreement that included provisions for profit-sharing, dispute resolution, and the process for handling a partner's departure. They also registered their trade name and ensured compliance with local zoning laws.

Example 2: Green Leaf Landscaping Rachel and Tim started a landscaping business called "Green Leaf Landscaping" as a general partnership. Their agreement detailed each partner's capital contribution, roles, and responsibilities. They included a contingency plan for business disruptions and a non-compete clause to protect their business from internal competition.

Example 3: Creative Solutions LLP Emma and Jack formed an LLP for their consulting business, "Creative Solutions." They used an escrow account to manage the transfer of ownership shares and included an indemnification clause to protect against liabilities. Their partnership agreement also covered amendments to reflect changes in business operations.

Conclusion

Understanding key legal vocabulary related to partnerships is essential for navigating and managing a partnership effectively. By familiarizing yourself with these terms, you can better understand your legal responsibilities, protect your interests, and ensure smooth business operations. This chapter provides a detailed look at important legal terms in the context of partnerships, with practical examples to help you grasp their meaning and application.

A CORPORATION: WHAT IT IS, ITS KEY CHARACTERISTICS, ADVANTAGES, AND DISADVANTAGES

Introduction

Understanding the concept of a corporation is essential for anyone interested in business or commercial law. In this chapter, we will explore what a corporation is, its key characteristics, advantages, and disadvantages, along with practical examples to illustrate how corporations operate. This guide is designed to be accessible for beginners, using simple language to explain complex concepts.

Understanding a Corporation

A **corporation** is a business structure that exists as a separate legal entity from its owners. This means that the corporation itself can enter into contracts, sue or be sued, and is responsible for its own debts and liabilities. Unlike sole proprietorships or partnerships, a corporation provides limited liability protection to its shareholders, meaning their personal assets are generally protected from the corporation's debts.

Key Characteristics:

- **Separate Legal Entity**: The corporation is legally distinct from its owners.
- **Limited Liability**: Shareholders are only liable up to the amount they have invested in the corporation.
- **Board of Directors**: The corporation is managed by a board of directors elected by the shareholders.
- **Shares of Stock**: Ownership in the corporation is represented by shares of stock.

Advantages of a Corporation

1. **Limited Liability**:
    - **Explanation**: Shareholders are not personally liable for the corporation's debts and obligations. Their risk is limited to their investment in the corporation.
    - **Example**: If Tech Innovations Inc. faces a lawsuit, the personal assets of its shareholders, including founder Jane, are protected. They are only at risk of losing the money they invested in the company.

2. **Perpetual Existence:**
   - **Explanation**: A corporation continues to exist even if the original owners leave or pass away. Ownership can be transferred through the sale of shares.
   - **Example**: Apple Inc. continues to operate despite changes in its leadership and ownership over the years, demonstrating the corporation's ability to outlast its founders and initial shareholders.
3. **Ease of Capital Acquisition:**
   - **Explanation**: Corporations can raise capital by issuing shares of stock, making it easier to secure large amounts of funding for growth and expansion.
   - **Example**: XYZ Corp. raised $10 million by selling shares to investors, which it used to expand its operations and develop new products.
4. **Transferability of Shares:**
   - **Explanation**: Shares of stock can be easily bought and sold, allowing for flexibility in ownership.
   - **Example**: John decided to sell his shares in ABC Corp. to invest in another venture, demonstrating the ease with which shareholders can change their investment portfolios.
5. **Credibility and Prestige:**
   - **Explanation**: Being incorporated can enhance a company's credibility and reputation, making it more attractive to investors, customers, and partners.
   - **Example**: Omega Corporation's status as an incorporated entity helped it secure contracts with major clients and attract top talent in the industry.

Disadvantages of a Corporation

1. **Complex Formation and Administration:**
   - **Explanation**: Establishing and maintaining a corporation involves more legal and administrative requirements than other business structures.

- **Example**: Forming Alpha Corp. required extensive paperwork, including drafting articles of incorporation and bylaws, and it must comply with ongoing regulatory requirements.

2. **Double Taxation**:
    - **Explanation**: Corporations are taxed on their profits, and shareholders are also taxed on any dividends they receive, leading to double taxation.
    - **Example**: Delta Inc. pays corporate taxes on its earnings, and when it distributes dividends to shareholders, those shareholders must also pay taxes on their dividend income.

3. **Costly to Maintain**:
    - **Explanation**: Corporations face higher costs for legal compliance, accounting, and administrative tasks.
    - **Example**: Gamma Corporation spends a significant amount on legal fees and regulatory compliance to ensure it meets all government requirements.

4. **Regulation and Compliance**:
    - **Explanation**: Corporations must adhere to strict government regulations and reporting standards, which can be burdensome.
    - **Example**: Epsilon Corp. is required to submit detailed financial reports to regulatory bodies, which adds to its administrative workload.

5. **Potential for Conflicts**:
    - **Explanation**: The separation of ownership and management can lead to conflicts between shareholders and directors.
    - **Example**: Shareholders of Zeta Inc. disagreed with the board of directors' decision to reinvest profits rather than distribute dividends, leading to tensions and disputes.

Practical Examples

Example 1: Tech Innovations Inc. Tech Innovations Inc. is a technology company that was incorporated to develop and sell innovative software solutions. As a corporation, it can raise significant capital by issuing shares, which it uses for research and development. The company's shareholders are protected by limited liability, meaning they are not personally responsible for the company's debts.

Example 2: HealthCare Co. HealthCare Co. is a healthcare corporation that provides medical services and products. It benefits from perpetual existence, allowing it to continue operations even as the original founders retire. The corporation has a board of directors that oversees the management of the business, ensuring continuity and stability.

Example 3: Creative Arts Corp. Creative Arts Corp. was established by a group of artists to market and sell their work. The corporation has enhanced their credibility and allowed them to secure larger contracts and collaborations. Despite facing complex regulatory requirements, the corporation's ability to raise capital and manage risk has enabled it to expand its operations significantly.

Conclusion

A corporation is a powerful business structure that offers significant advantages, including limited liability, ease of raising capital, and perpetual existence. However, it also comes with complexities, such as higher costs and regulatory requirements. Understanding these aspects is crucial for anyone considering forming a corporation or investing in one. This chapter provides a detailed overview of corporations, including their benefits and challenges, with practical examples to help you understand how they operate.

A CONVERSATION BETWEEN A LAWYER AND A CLIENT WHO IS CONSIDERING STARTING A CORPORATION FOR THEIR NEW BUSINESS

Introduction

Forming a corporation can offer significant benefits, including limited liability and easier access to capital. In this chapter, we will present a conversation between a lawyer and a client who is considering starting a corporation for their new business. We will analyze the dialogue in simple English, ensuring it is accessible for beginners. This will provide clear explanations and practical examples to help you understand the process of forming a corporation and the legal considerations involved.

The Conversation

Context: The following conversation is between a lawyer and a client who is seeking advice on forming a corporation for a new business venture. The dialogue highlights important aspects and benefits of establishing a corporation.

LAWYER: Good morning, Mr. Thompson. How can I assist you today?

CLIENT: Good morning, Ms. Davis. I'm planning to start a new business and I'm considering forming a corporation. I'd like some advice on whether this is the right choice.

LAWYER: Certainly. Can you tell me more about your business idea?

CLIENT: Sure. I want to start a tech company that develops smart home devices. We expect rapid growth and will need significant capital to fund research and production.

LAWYER: That sounds like a promising venture. Will you be the sole owner, or are you planning to bring in other investors or partners?

CLIENT: I'm planning to have several co-founders, and we're also looking to attract investors to raise capital.

LAWYER: Given your plans for growth and the need for substantial capital, forming a corporation could be a suitable option. It will allow you to issue shares and bring in investors while limiting your personal liability.

CLIENT: That's good to know. Can you explain how forming a corporation will limit my personal liability?

LAWYER: As a corporation is a separate legal entity, it is responsible for its own debts and obligations. This means that as a shareholder, you are only liable up to the amount you have invested in the corporation. Your personal assets are protected.

CLIENT: That's reassuring. What about the process of forming a corporation? Is it complicated?

LAWYER: It involves a few steps, including drafting and filing articles of incorporation, creating bylaws, appointing directors, and issuing stock. It can be a bit more complex than setting up a sole proprietorship, but I can help guide you through each step.

CLIENT: That sounds manageable. Are there any other advantages to forming a corporation that I should be aware of?

LAWYER: Yes, in addition to limited liability and easier access to capital, a corporation has perpetual existence, meaning it can continue to operate regardless of changes in ownership. It also adds credibility and can attract higher levels of talent and customers.

CLIENT: That's helpful. Are there any downsides or challenges with forming a corporation?

LAWYER: The main challenges are the initial cost and the ongoing regulatory requirements. Corporations are subject to double taxation, where profits are taxed at the corporate level and again when distributed as dividends to shareholders. Additionally, maintaining a corporation requires more administrative work and compliance with various regulations.

CLIENT: I see. We're prepared for the additional work if it means we can grow our business and protect our personal assets. Can you help us with the paperwork?

LAWYER: Absolutely. I can assist with drafting the necessary documents and ensuring you meet all legal requirements. We'll need details about your business structure and the roles of each founder.

CLIENT: Great. Let's proceed with forming the corporation. We'll provide the details you need.

LAWYER: Excellent. I'll start preparing the documents. Let's schedule a follow-up meeting to finalize everything.

CLIENT: Sounds good. Thank you for your help, Ms. Davis.

LAWYER: You're welcome, Mr. Thompson. I look forward to working with you on your new venture.

Detailed Breakdown

1. **Business Idea and Scope**:
    - **Explanation**: The client, Mr. Thompson, is planning to start a tech company that will develop smart home devices, requiring substantial capital and planning for rapid growth.
    - **Example**: Similar to how Jane started a software company focused on developing innovative applications, Mr. Thompson's tech company will need significant investment and strategic planning for expansion.

2. **Ownership and Investment Plans**:
    - **Explanation**: The client intends to have co-founders and attract investors, making a corporation an ideal choice for raising capital and managing multiple stakeholders.
    - **Example**: John and Lisa formed a corporation to open a chain of restaurants, allowing them to bring in investors and share ownership while maintaining a professional structure.

3. **Limited Liability**:
    - **Explanation**: The lawyer explains that a corporation provides limited liability, protecting the personal assets of shareholders from business debts and legal issues.
    - **Example**: If Sarah's corporation faces a lawsuit, her personal savings and property are not at risk, only her investment in the company is, which gives her financial security.

4. **Process of Forming a Corporation**:
    - **Explanation**: The process involves drafting articles of incorporation, creating bylaws, appointing directors, and issuing stock, which can be more complex than forming other business structures.

- **Example**: Mark and Rachel went through a detailed process of incorporating their tech startup, which included filing legal documents and setting up a formal board of directors.

5. **Advantages of a Corporation**:
    - **Explanation**: The lawyer highlights benefits such as limited liability, easier access to capital, perpetual existence, and added credibility, which can attract investors and customers.
    - **Example**: Emma and Jack formed a corporation for their consulting firm, which helped them secure large contracts and attract top talent, enhancing their business growth.

6. **Challenges of a Corporation**:
    - **Explanation**: The main challenges include higher initial costs, ongoing regulatory requirements, double taxation, and the need for more administrative work.
    - **Example**: Alex and Maria faced challenges with the regulatory requirements and double taxation of their corporation, but they managed these with the help of professional advisors.

7. **Commitment to Proceed**:
    - **Explanation**: The client is willing to proceed with forming the corporation, understanding the advantages and being prepared to handle the additional work involved.
    - **Example**: Similar to John and Lisa, who committed to forming a corporation for their restaurant chain, Mr. Thompson is ready to proceed with his tech company, understanding the long-term benefits.

Practical Insights

Evaluating the Business Structure:

- **Why It's Important**: Choosing the right business structure is crucial for managing liabilities, raising capital, and ensuring long-term growth. A corporation offers significant advantages for businesses planning substantial growth and investment.
- **Example**: John and Lisa chose a corporation for their restaurant chain, enabling them to bring in investors and manage growth efficiently.

Understanding Legal and Financial Responsibilities:

- **Key Considerations**: Understanding the legal and financial responsibilities of a corporation helps in planning for compliance, managing taxes, and protecting personal assets.
- **Example**: Mark and Rachel, starting a tech company, prepared for the legal and financial complexities of running a corporation by consulting with legal and financial advisors.

Preparing for Challenges:

- **Implications**: Being aware of potential challenges, such as regulatory compliance and double taxation, helps in planning strategies to address these issues and maintain business stability.
- **Example**: Sarah and David, running a consulting firm, planned for the additional administrative and tax obligations of their corporation, ensuring they met all requirements and managed their finances effectively.

Conclusion

Understanding the process and benefits of forming a corporation is essential for businesses looking to grow and protect personal assets. By considering key factors such as limited liability, ease of capital acquisition, and regulatory requirements, you can make informed decisions about whether a corporation is the right structure for your business. Listening to professional advice and preparing thoroughly for the legal and financial aspects of a corporation are crucial steps in establishing a successful business.

EXPLORE THE KEY BENEFITS AND CHALLENGES OF FORMING A CORPORATION

Introduction

Understanding the advantages and disadvantages of corporations is crucial for anyone considering this business structure. In this chapter, we will explore the key benefits and challenges of forming a corporation, using simple language and practical examples to make these concepts accessible for beginners. This guide aims to provide a clear and comprehensive overview of what makes a corporation a unique and powerful business entity.

What is a Corporation?

A **corporation** is a business entity created by law, with its own legal identity separate from its owners. This means that a corporation can own assets, incur liabilities, and enter into contracts independently of its shareholders. It offers limited liability protection to its owners, known as shareholders, who risk only their investment in the corporation.

Key Characteristics:

- **Separate Legal Entity**: The corporation exists independently of its owners.
- **Limited Liability**: Shareholders are protected from personal liability for corporate debts.
- **Perpetual Existence**: The corporation continues to exist even if the original owners leave or pass away.
- **Transferability of Shares**: Ownership can be easily transferred through the sale of shares.

Advantages of Corporations

1. **Limited Liability:**
    - **Explanation**: Shareholders are only liable for the amount they have invested in the corporation. Personal assets are protected from the corporation's debts and legal obligations.
    - **Example**: If XYZ Corp. is sued, the shareholders, including John who owns 100 shares, are not personally responsible for paying the lawsuit settlement. Their risk is limited to the value of their shares.

2. **Ease of Raising Capital:**
    - **Explanation:** Corporations can raise significant amounts of capital by issuing shares of stock, which attracts investors and helps finance expansion.
    - **Example:** Tech Innovations Inc. raised $5 million by issuing new shares, which allowed them to develop new products and expand their market presence.
3. **Perpetual Existence:**
    - **Explanation:** A corporation can continue to operate indefinitely, regardless of changes in ownership or management.
    - **Example:** Alpha Corp. has been in business for over 50 years, outlasting its original founders and several generations of shareholders.
4. **Attracting Talent:**
    - **Explanation:** Corporations can attract highly qualified individuals to serve on their board of directors and management team, enhancing the business's expertise and credibility.
    - **Example:** Beta Corp. attracted a renowned CEO to lead their company, boosting investor confidence and driving business growth.
5. **Transferability of Ownership:**
    - **Explanation:** Shares of a corporation can be easily bought and sold, making it simple for shareholders to transfer ownership without disrupting business operations.
    - **Example:** Emily sold her shares in Creative Solutions Corp. to invest in a new venture, allowing her to easily change her investment focus.
6. **Tax Advantages:**
    - **Explanation:** Corporations may benefit from tax deductions for business expenses, potentially lowering their overall tax liability.
    - **Example:** Delta Inc. deducted expenses for research and development, reducing their taxable income and saving on taxes.

Disadvantages of Corporations

1. **Complex Formation and Administration:**
    - **Explanation**: Forming a corporation requires more time, effort, and money compared to other business structures due to the need for detailed legal documents and regulatory compliance.
    - **Example**: Forming Epsilon Corp. involved drafting articles of incorporation, creating bylaws, and filing with the state, incurring significant legal fees and administrative costs.

2. **Double Taxation:**
    - **Explanation**: Corporate profits are taxed twice—once at the corporate level and again as shareholder dividends.
    - **Example**: Gamma Inc. paid corporate taxes on its earnings, and shareholders like Sarah had to pay personal taxes on the dividends they received, leading to double taxation.

3. **Regulatory Compliance:**
    - **Explanation**: Corporations must adhere to strict government regulations and reporting requirements, which can be costly and time-consuming.
    - **Example**: Omega Corp. spent substantial resources on compliance with federal and state regulations, including filing annual reports and maintaining detailed financial records.

4. **Loss of Control:**
    - **Explanation**: The separation of ownership and management can result in shareholders losing direct control over the company, which is managed by a board of directors.
    - **Example**: Jane, a founder of Beta Corp., no longer has day-to-day control over business decisions, which are now made by the board of directors.

5. **Increased Costs:**
    - **Explanation**: Corporations face higher costs for formation, legal compliance, and ongoing operations compared to sole proprietorships or partnerships.

- **Example**: Zeta Corp. incurred significant legal and administrative costs to maintain its corporate status and comply with ongoing regulatory requirements.

6. **Potential for Conflicts**:
   - **Explanation**: Differences between shareholders and directors or among shareholders themselves can lead to conflicts, particularly regarding the direction and management of the corporation.
   - **Example**: Shareholders of Theta Inc. disagreed with the board's decision to reinvest profits instead of paying dividends, leading to internal disputes.

Practical Examples

Example 1: Tech Innovations Inc. Tech Innovations Inc. is a corporation that specializes in developing smart home technology. By issuing shares, the company raised $10 million in capital, which allowed them to expand their product line and enter new markets. The shareholders enjoy limited liability, protecting their personal assets from the company's debts.

Example 2: Health Solutions Corp. Health Solutions Corp. is a healthcare company that provides medical services and products. It benefits from perpetual existence, allowing it to continue operations despite changes in ownership. The corporation's ability to attract top medical professionals has enhanced its reputation and driven growth.

Example 3: Green Energy Corp. Green Energy Corp. was formed to develop renewable energy solutions. The corporation faced significant regulatory compliance costs but benefited from the ability to raise capital through stock sales. The company's shareholders appreciate the limited liability protection, which shields their personal assets from business risks.

Conclusion

Corporations offer substantial benefits, including limited liability, ease of raising capital, and perpetual existence, making them an attractive option for businesses seeking growth and stability. However, they also come with challenges such as complex formation, double taxation, and increased regulatory compliance. Understanding these advantages and disadvantages is essential for making informed decisions about whether a corporation is the right structure for your business.

CONCLUSION

As we conclude our journey through *"Mastering Commercial Law: Your Ultimate Guide to Understanding Key Business Structures and Terms Related To Sole Proprietorships, Partnerships, and Corporations Like A Pro In Minutes,"* we hope you feel empowered and equipped with the essential knowledge to navigate the complexities of commercial law with confidence and clarity.

Summary of Key Takeaways

1. **Comprehensive Understanding of Business Structures**:
   - You now have a solid grasp of the differences between sole proprietorships, partnerships, and corporations. Each structure comes with its own set of benefits and challenges, and you are now equipped to make informed decisions about which is best for your business needs.

2. **Mastery of Legal Vocabulary**:
   - With a newfound fluency in key legal terms, you can confidently engage in discussions, negotiations, and legal processes. The once-intimidating jargon of commercial law is now a tool in your arsenal, enabling you to protect your interests and those of your business.

3. **Practical Insights and Real-World Applications**:
   - By exploring real-world examples and case studies, you've seen how the concepts discussed in this book play out in actual business scenarios. These insights provide you with a practical framework to apply your knowledge effectively in your own business ventures.

4. **Critical Questions for Business Success**:
   - The critical questions posed throughout this guide have helped you think deeply about your business choices. They serve as a roadmap, guiding you through the essential considerations for building a robust legal foundation for your business.

Moving Forward: Applying Your Knowledge

Knowledge is only powerful when applied. Now that you've mastered the basics of commercial law, it's time to put your learning into action. Here's how you can take the next steps:

1. **Evaluate Your Business Structure**:

- Assess your current or planned business structure in light of what you've learned. Determine if it aligns with your business goals and provides the legal and financial protections you need. If changes are necessary, you now have the knowledge to make informed decisions and implement them effectively.

2. **Engage in Informed Legal Discussions**:
    - Use your newfound legal vocabulary to confidently participate in discussions with legal professionals, partners, and stakeholders. Clear communication is key to negotiating favorable terms and protecting your interests.

3. **Develop Strong Legal Foundations**:
    - Apply the principles and practical insights from this book to draft or revise key legal documents. Whether it's setting up a new corporation, creating a partnership agreement, or understanding the legal implications of your business choices, you are now equipped to lay a strong legal foundation for your business.

4. **Seek Continued Learning and Professional Advice**:
    - Commercial law is a dynamic field. Stay informed about changes in regulations and legal requirements that may impact your business. Don't hesitate to seek professional legal advice when necessary to ensure your business remains compliant and protected.

Embrace Your Legal Confidence

As you close this book, remember that the knowledge you've gained is a powerful tool. Use it to navigate the legal landscape with confidence and to make informed decisions that will propel your business toward success. You have the ability to protect your interests, seize opportunities, and steer your business with a strong legal foundation.

Take the first step today. Reassess your business structure, refine your legal strategies, and apply the insights you've gained to build a business that is not only successful but legally sound.

Thank you for choosing to embark on this journey with us. We wish you the best of success in your business endeavors and look forward to seeing you thrive with the confidence and knowledge you have gained from mastering commercial law.

CHECK OUT OTHER BOOKS

Go here to check out other related books that might interest you:

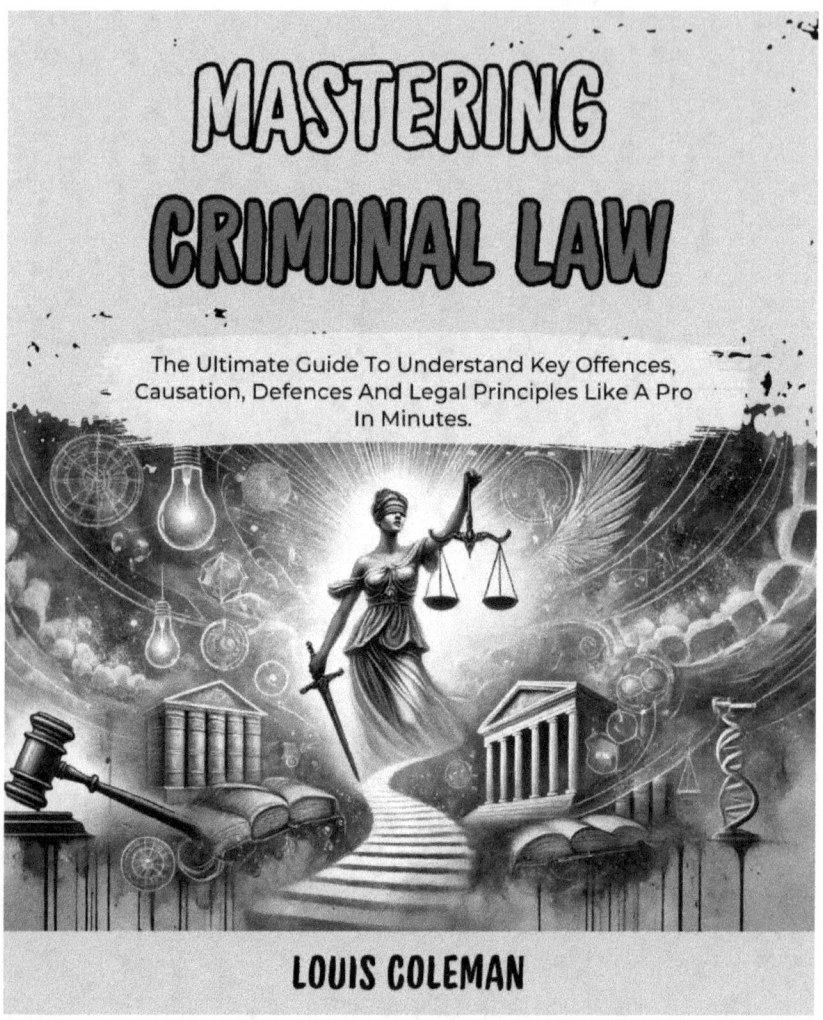

Mastering Criminal Law: The Ultimate Guide To Understand Key Offences, Causation, Defences And Legal Principles Like A Pro In Minutes.

https://www.amazon.com/dp/B0D4H97Y7B

Mastering Academic Legal Writing: A Step-By-Step Guide, Proven Techniques, Tips And Strategies For Crafting Powerful And Compelling Legal Documents Like A Pro In Minutes.

https://www.amazon.com/dp/B0D7J6FNTY

Mastering Business Writing: A Step-By-Step Guide, Proven Techniques, Tips & Strategies For Crafting Powerful And Compelling Business Letters, Reports, Proposals and Emails Like A Pro In Minutes.

https://www.amazon.com/dp/B0D7N1Y8VM

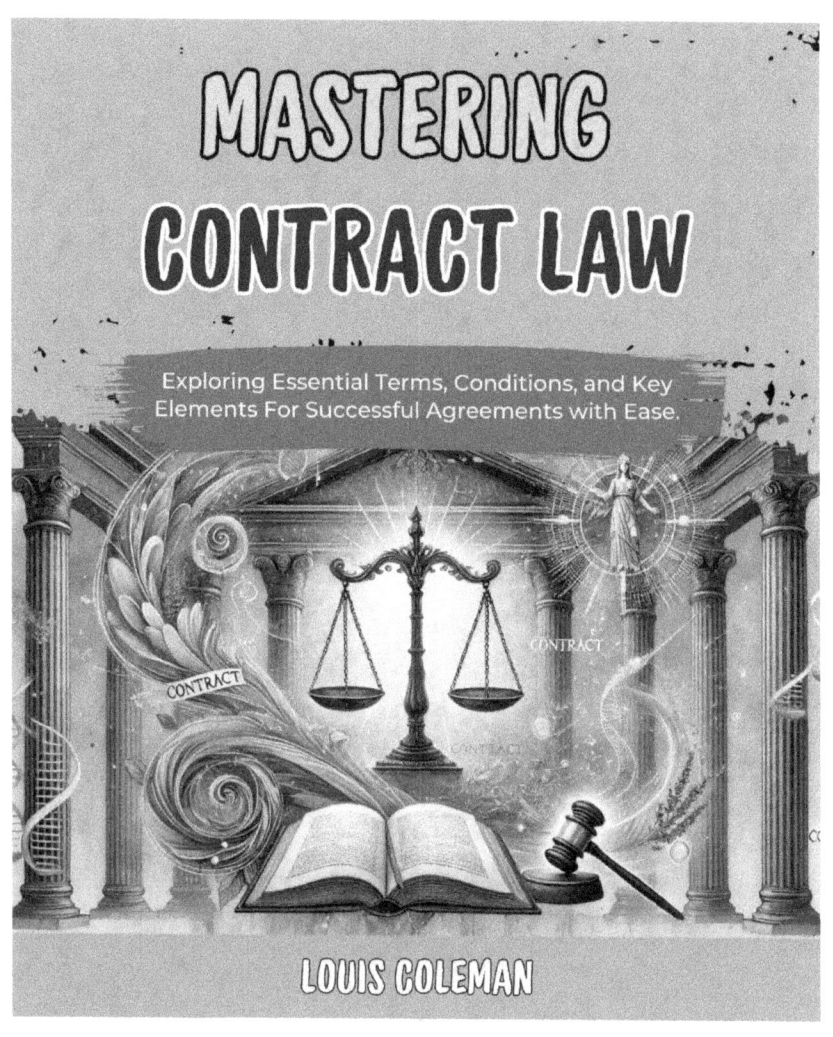

Mastering Contract Law: Exploring Essential Terms, Conditions, and Key Elements For Successful Agreements with Ease.

https://www.amazon.com/dp/B0D7Q6QRF5

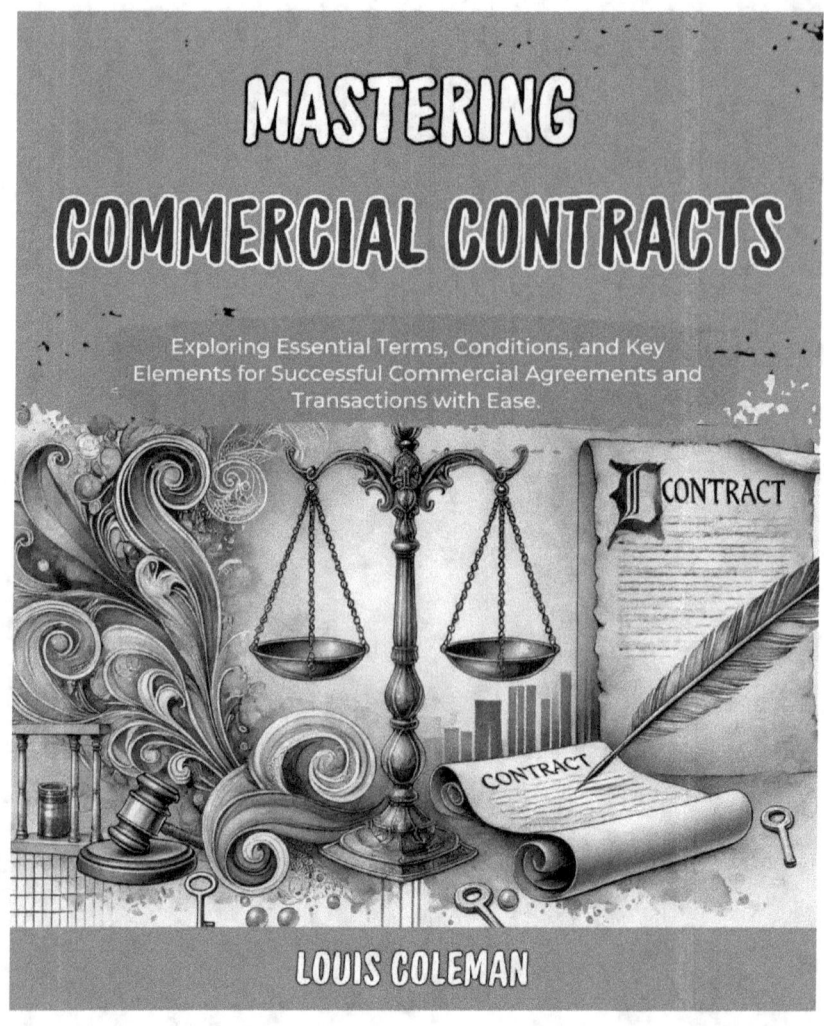

Mastering Commercial Contracts: Exploring Essential Terms, Conditions, and Key Elements For Successful Commercial Agreements and Transactions with Ease.

https://www.amazon.com/dp/B0D7TRSYLM

Kindle Publishing Guidelines: The Ultimate Guide, Tips, Tricks, Secrets On How To Generate A Huge Passive Income With Your Own Books Within A Short Period Of Time.

https://www.amazon.com/dp/B0CW1MJXDW

Cryptocurrency Investment Strategies: A Step By Step Guide, Tips, Tricks, Secrets And Strategies To Invest Successfully And Become A Millionaire In Cryptocurrency.

https://www.amazon.com/dp/B0D7611C9C

Design Like A Pro With Canva: The Step By Step Canva Guide To Create Professional Graphics And Transform Your Designs Instantly.

https://www.amazon.com/dp/B0D6FDQZKF

Canva Mastery For Beginners: The Complete Canva Expert Guide To Design Everything With Ease And Fast Like A Pro.

https://www.amazon.com/dp/B0D2VXN8KB

Crack Ielts Speaking Part 1: Proven Secrets, Tips and Strategies On How To Achieve An 8.0+ Band Score in Ielts Speaking Part 1 Easily.

https://www.amazon.com/dp/B0CYB14RFW

Crack Ielts Writing Task 2: Excellent Sample Answers By Topics, Tips and Strategies On How To Achieve An 8.0+ Band Score in Ielts Writing Task 2 Easily.

https://www.amazon.com/dp/B0CXJSNZSG

Ielts Speaking Part 1 By Topics: Over 200 Excellent Sample Answers By Topics You Must Know To Achieve An 8.0+ Band Score In Ielts Speaking Part 1 Easily.

https://www.amazon.com/dp/B0D2VWJHDR

Ielts Speaking Part 2 By Topics: Over 100 Excellent Sample Answers By Topics You Must Know To Achieve An 8.0+ Band Score In Ielts Speaking Part 2 Easily.

https://www.amazon.com/dp/B0D2S5ZDP6

Mastering IELTS Speaking: Achieve Band 8.0+ in Ielts Speaking with Proven Strategies, Excellent Sample Answers and Practice Exercises.

https://www.amazon.com/dp/B0CW6C9HK8

Mastering Ielts Writing: Achieve Band 8.0+ in Ielts Writing with Proven Strategies, Excellent Sample Answers and Practice Exercises.

https://www.amazon.com/dp/B0D4TD1NLC

Ielts Writing For Success: The Complete Guide To Achieve Band 8.0+ In Ielts Writing With Proven Strategies, Vocabulary & Excellent Sample Answers In 2 Weeks.

https://www.amazon.com/dp/B0D4W6JVRR

Mastering Ielts Reading: Achieve Band 8.0+ Easily in Ielts Reading with Proven Strategies, Tips, Tricks and Techniques.

https://www.amazon.com/dp/B0D2BJZBS8

www.ingramcontent.com/pod-product-compliance
Lightning Source LLC
Chambersburg PA
CBHW071836210526
45479CB00001B/169